SEVENTH-DAY ADVENTISTS:
CULT OR CHRISTIANS?

BY WALTER C. THOMPSON, M.D.

ISBN 0-9628512-1-3

Foreword

In the last twenty years I have been involved in large public evangelistic meetings. Thousands have attended throughout the United States, Europe, and Asia. Often when attendees learn that I am a Seventh-day Adventist they ask, "Is the Seventh-day Adventist Church a cult?" Today people are afraid to get involved in something they don't know about or understand. They are skeptical. They don't want to be taken in or to be deceived. This natural caution leads many to avoid discovering new truth.

Dr. Walter Thompson, a personal friend of mine, who has traveled with me throughout Europe and Asia for public evangelistic meetings, effectively addresses the question, "Is the Seventh-day Adventist Church a cult?" His book clearly reveals the Christ-centered nature of Adventism. He is genuinely honest. His transparency shines through every page. Dr. Thompson is a surgeon. He is not a paid employee of the Seventh-day Adventist Church. He writes from the depth of his own personal spiritual experience.

As I read Dr. Thompson's book I was excited about it. I felt as if I was taking a journey with a friend, experiencing with him a quest for truth. If you are a sincere seeker after truth, if your heart and mind are open to the truth, if you are seeking for the Spirit's direction in your life, this book is for you.

Dr. Thompson deals with the core of Adventism effectively. He is not an advertiser trying to sell a product. He is rather a genuine, sincere Christian believing that he has discovered facets of truth that are absolutely essential to share with a shattered world approaching the second millennium.

As you read, I am certain the same Spirit that has guided Dr. Thompson in his pilgrimage will guide you in yours.

MARK FINLEY

Table of Contents

Preface 1

Introduction 2

A Brief History of the Seventh-day Adventist Church 3

Chapter I   Seventh-Day Adventism:
Its Reason for Existence 5

Chapter II   A World Awakened, A People Born:
The Beginnings of Adventism 11

Chapter III   The War To End All Wars:
The Battle Between Good and Evil 15

Chapter IV   The Judgment 23

Chapter V   Legalism: Keepers of the Law 33

Chapter VI   The Sabbath: Sign of the Father 43

Chapter VII   Modern-day Prophet 53

Chapter VII   The Health Message 59

Chapter IX   Dead or Alive?: What Happens
at the Time of Death? 65

Chapter X   End-Time Events 71

Chapter XI   With Liberty and Justice for All:
Separation of Church and State 81

Chapter XII   Worship the Creator—Creation vs. Evolution:
The Adventist Position 83

Chapter XIII   The Paradox of Adventism:
The Author's Testimony 87

Bibliography 93

Preface

Seventh-day Adventists are sometimes considered to be a cult. As a consequence of the cult designation, or perhaps because of the beliefs that lead to that designation in the first place, the unique contributions that Adventists might otherwise make to religious thought and action are often lost to the world. As the gulf separating the Adventist community from the expanding ecumenical movement widens, it may be expected that the "cult" designation will gain increasing expression. Because of this, it becomes increasingly important that the teachings of the Adventist people be clearly presented in order for interested individuals to accurately evaluate their validity and thereby make their own determinations.

This book is written in response to this need. It is my desire to paint as accurate a picture as possible in a limited space. I shall attempt to be objective and deal honestly with the issues discussed. My intent is not primarily to make converts to the Adventist faith, but instead to inform. If, in the process of study, some reader should be impressed with the beauty of the message and come to share in its blessings, I would consider my effort more than adequately rewarded. Could any Christian feel otherwise?

I am a Seventh-day Adventist Christian. I was raised by an Adventist mother and received some of my education in Adventist schools. My early education allowed me the privilege of learning the rudiments of the faith in the nurturing atmosphere of the Church. My later medical training provided ample opportunity to test the tenets of my church. In subsequent years of service to the needs of the sick and those in pain in several lands I have been further blessed as Christians and non-Christians alike have shared with me their joys and their sorrows, their faith and their frustrations, their hopes and their despair, and I have been forced to examine over and over again the principles of my own faith.

I am not a theologian. Theological terms are foreign to my pen. Although by training I am a physician and surgeon, the Bible has always been a primary text of study for me. My inquiring mind has often pushed me beyond fatigue in its search for knowledge and understanding. Few stones have been left unturned, few prospects of truth left undisturbed. I believe that my life experience has permitted me to gain familiarity with the mainstream of Adventist thought as well as with many of its fringes.

As a lay member of the Adventist church, I am not bound by all of the same cautions and restrictions that an official representative of the church might be although I strive for sensitivity to their interests. (For a more comprehensive description of Adventist doctrines, see *Seventh-day Adventists Believe . . .*, p. 27.) From my vantage point, I am free to express certain words and concepts that, for fear of offending other Christians, the official representatives of the church might find wise to avoid. I shall try to express these concepts accurately and in accord with historical Adventist understanding. Occasionally, I will point out differences that exist between our stated beliefs and our actions. I do this to explain the sometimes double messages that those looking at us may receive as they study our doctrines and observe our actions, a point which I believe to be critical if one is to gain a clear understanding of true Adventist thought.

May the spirit of God instruct each reader as he studies the pages of this book, to the glory of the God of our creation.

1

Introduction:
Definition of a Cult

Webster defines "cult" as a system of religious forms, ceremonies, and rites. The word is derived from the Latin "cultus," or "colere," meaning to cultivate or worship.

According to this broad definition, any gathering of people for the purpose of worship may properly be referred to as a "cult." Indeed, in some cultures, the word is used this way. But this is not true in our society. Instead, in practice here, the term is most often used descriptively to identify religious groups that believe and teach concepts outside the generally accepted norm for orthodox Christianity as seen in the major Catholic and Protestant denominations. Frequently, the word "cult" is used in a pejorative sense, implying (if not stating outright) that the group labeled "cult" is dangerous and ought to be denounced or at least avoided. The experience at Jonestown, Guyana, in November, 1978, served well to emphasize this sense of the word "cult."

Several doctrinal teachings serve to identify Christian orthodoxy even though many variations exist. These teachings include the triune nature of God, the saving work of grace through Jesus Christ, the authority of Scripture, the nature of man, and the punishment of the wicked. In contrast, "cults" may either reject some or all of these tenets, or interpret them differently.

Besides their differences in belief, cult groups often have characteristics that tend to create a wall of separation between them and other people. This distancing may be the result of the way the group views itself, or the result of the way it is viewed by those outside the group.

In order for any new group to organize and grow to a point of recognition, there must be strong leadership. Often, this is one individual. Sometimes, by his own design or because of power granted him by his followers because of his leadership qualities or personal charisma, he is exalted to a position high above mere humanity. When this happens, the door is open for all sorts of dangerous and destructive practices. (We have witnessed some of these in this generation.) But strong leaders do not arise "de novo," or without a cause. Most cults generate in response to stress and unrest within the greater society. Although this response may be either genuinely constructive or downright destructive, the effect may be the same. Anything that threatens the status quo, whatever the desire or intent of the instigator, creates a defensive reaction against that threat. The reciprocal effect of this is not without its own reaction among the members of the group who are now positioned in an adversarial stance. At times this is expressed in aggressive ways.

A number of the teachings of Seventh-day Adventists are of such a nature that the "cult" designation has been applied by some critics. Are they correct in their assessment? It is my hope that this book will equip the reader with the information necessary to make that determination for himself.

A Brief History of the Seventh-day Adventist Church

The Seventh-day Adventist church was born and nurtured in the early years of the nineteenth century. It arose out of the frustration and turmoil that followed a misinterpretation of prophetic Scripture in which a man, William Miller, predicted the end of the world and the return of Christ in 1844.

A number of prominent individuals played major roles in the formation and early development of the church. Among them was one Ellen Harmon, a young lady who through her alleged prophetic inspiration gave counsel and direction to the emerging organization. That inspiration was destined to influence the organization's subsequent direction in history.

The church was organized under the descriptive name "Seventh-day Adventist" in 1863 with several hundred members in the New England area. It has prospered and experienced fairly steady growth in membership. It now numbers in the millions worldwide.

The Church's structure consists of a strong central organization—the General Conference—that oversees world divisions, unions, conferences, and local congregations. All are united in serving the central purpose and work of the organization. Its work, described as proclaiming the last-day emphasis of the "everlasting Gospel" to the whole world in preparation for the return of Jesus as King of Kings and Lord of Lords, transcends the organization itself to include many lay persons in individual and group ministries.

Education, health care, and welfare relief services combine within the church with literature sales and distribution, radio and television evangelism, seminars and lecture series, as well as small group Bible studies, in a concerted effort to fulfill the mission to the world. These have not been without effect. Adventists are recognized in many circles for their quality health care, their attractive literature, effective public media presentations, balanced education, and compassionate welfare ministry. Yet, in spite of this general overall acclaim for quality, they remain for the most part excluded from the larger circle of Christian activity. At times this exclusion is the result of their conscious choice to avoid close alliances to other organizations that might tie their hands or otherwise hinder them in their perceived role of proclaiming their distinctive end-time message. At other times, Adventists are excluded from active participation in certain functions that might enhance their mission because of their "unorthodox" doctrinal teachings. For many, this apparent paradox of a people living quality lives and making significant positive contributions to the good of society while espousing "untenable beliefs" is beyond comprehension.

In the pages that follow I will attempt to put this paradox into proper perspective. I will describe some of the unique features of Adventist thought that Adventists believe constitute the reason for their existence. I will discuss their sometimes distinctive doctrinal beliefs along with selected supporting Scriptural references. Where indicated, in order to emphasize or explain a point, I will compare their beliefs with views held by other Christians and religious people. It is not my intention to criticize or condemn the religious convictions of others, nor to suggest that Adventists are in any way superior to other people. I do believe, however, that the Adventist church was born of divine appointment to proclaim a distinctive message to a hurting and dying world. To the extent that my promotion of this concept may challenge the more popular dogmas of other religious systems, I must accept responsibility for my actions.

It is my sincere desire that the reader will reserve judgment regarding the "cult" nature of Adventism until he has had the opportunity to read and study the whole argument along with its supporting Scriptures and references. Then, whether his prayerful consideration is one of espousal or of rejection, it will be an informed judgment and in keeping with the freedom of mind granted to us by our Maker.

REFERENCE

Seventh-day Adventists Believe. *Hagerstown, MD: Review and Herald Publishing Association, 1988.*

Chapter I

Seventh-day Adventism: Its Reason for Existence

Any meaningful understanding of Adventism must include a study of its reason for existence. The Christian church has been around for hundreds of years. It has prestige, power, and influence. Many people feel that it would be an even greater power in the world if it were not so fragmented. In the face of such conditions, why does the Adventist church exist? How does it view its role in modern Christianity? Did it arise by the appointment of God, or is it a tool in the hands of Satan intent upon destroying the work of God among men?

Most Adventists are very much aware of their reason for existence. For many, there is only one reason. It is to proclaim the last invitation—the last warning message—of a loving God to a dying world in preparation for the return of Christ. That message reaches to the ends of the earth. It is for all people of every race, color, creed, and social group (1).

Traditionally, Adventists have not looked upon themselves as another church competing with other churches, but rather as a movement among Christendom with a single purpose, chosen by God to perform a specific task through the power of the Holy Spirit.

They think of the Advent Movement as the fulfillment of the Old Testament prophecy of Malachi which refers to the coming of the prophet Elijah before the great and terrible day of the Lord. They recognize that John the Baptist partially fulfilled this prophecy, preparing the way for Jesus' sojourn among men (2), but they believe that the prophecy has a secondary application in preparing the world for the Second Coming of Christ and the final judgment hour—for it is spoken of as the "Great and Terrible Day" (3).

As Elijah was commissioned to lead his nation from apostasy back to God, so Adventists believe they must serve a similar function in calling a people out of "Babylon" in preparation for Christ's return (4).

It is upon this basis, this sense of special purpose, upon this urgency of the times in which they live, that many of the teachings of the Adventist faith take root.

1. *Matthew 24:14 (New English Bible):* "And this gospel of the Kingdom will be proclaimed throughout the earth as a testimony to all nations; and then the end will come."

2. *Matthew 17:12 (NEB):* "But I tell you that Elijah has already come, and they failed to recognize him, and worked their will upon him; and in the same way the Son of Man is to suffer at their hands."

3. *Malachi 4:5 (NEB):* "Look, I will send you the Prophet Elijah before the great and terrible day of the Lord comes."

4. *Revelation 18:4 (NEB):* "Then I heard another voice from heaven that said: 'Come out of her, my people, lest you take part in her sins and share in her plagues.'"

5

Jesus was asked by His disciples why it was that the disciples of John fasted and lived such austere lives while Jesus and His disciples did not. Jesus' response was essentially that one cannot rejoice when the bridegroom is away, but when he comes, the rejoicing cannot be contained (5).

Adventists believe as did John the Baptist that this is not a time for frivolous living, for a whole order of creation has been taken in by the deceptions of the Evil One. The consequences of sin (i.e., sorrow, pain, sadness and death) wrack the human race. Evil has now almost completely replaced good in the human heart. Man has divorced himself nearly completely from God and from the blessings God would love to pour out upon him.

Soon, the cup of God's wrath will be full in a world that can no longer be touched by His love because its people have rejected Him and have chosen other lovers. Soon, man will reap the final consequence of being separated from God (6, 7).

In view of this urgency, Adventists believe that it is not a time for "business as usual." Instead, it is a time for uniting under the banner of Christ in the conflict between good and evil. A time to "put on the full armor of God" (Ephesians 6:11) so that, as valiant soldiers in His cause, the world might be given a true picture of His infinite love and a warning to turn and escape the high cost of sin. It is a time for believers to place all—all of their personal ambition, their lustful desire, and their self-centered concern—on the altar as a living sacrifice to God.

For, Our Father is not willing that anyone should die (8).

Seventh-day Adventists view it as a high privilege as sons and daughters of God to share with Him in His last great thrust, His last great battle, to win those whom he has created and redeemed back into harmony with His plan of life.

This is the motive, the driving force that from the beginning has created the life blood of the Adventist faith. This, in the Adventist view, is the reason to exist.

Such a faith quite naturally creates a response. To profess to believe in something and not respond is either to lie or to commit suicide. What the Spirit drives cannot be safely contained. Let us look at some of these responses Adventists have made.

6

Adventists believe in the value of education. True education, they believe, prepares people to live in harmony with the principles of God's government and the laws of His universe. They believe that the foundation stones of such education are found in the Holy Scriptures, in the book of nature, and in the book of God's providence. Such education is best begun in the Christian home with Christian parents (9).

As a child matures, Christ-centered schools must take over and expand from this important beginning. Accordingly, many Adventists begin the education of their children in their own homes and advance them on to Christian schools as they mature sufficiently to profit by such advancement.

Likewise, the Adventist community has developed schools that extend from kindergarten through professional training designed to prepare youth to serve in the cause of Christ both at home and in foreign lands. These schools, although offering a broad range of educational experience, have through the years emphasized preparing people to serve as teachers, ministers, and as servants in the various branches of the medical profession.

Adventists believe this is in keeping with the example that Jesus Himself set while a man upon earth—an example of meeting people where they were, of healing their wounds and then of bidding them to come and follow Him.

They believe also that the human mind is the channel of communication between God and man. Since this line of communication is so vital, they believe that it must be protected at all costs. Assaults either from within or without must be defeated. So far as lifestyle practices (diet, exercies, etc.) impact upon the physiological function of the human brain, they must be subjected to the controlling power of the Holy Spirit.

Alcohol, nicotine, caffeine, and all mind-altering drugs exert negative impacts and have no place in Adventist life except possibly under rare circumstances for their therapeutic effect (10).

Of equal importance to the physiological function is the content of data programmed into the mind computer from which it can draw in its communication with both God and man. Adventists believe in the axiom, "By beholding, we become changed," as a principle well-established in brain physiology and confirmed in Scripture (II Corinthians 3:18; 4:6). They argue that

9. Education *by Ellen White*:
pp. 15-16: "To restore in man the image of his Maker, to bring him back to the perfection in which he was created, to promote the development of body, mind, and soul, that the divine purpose in his creation might be realized—this was to be the work of redemption. This is the object of education, the great object of life ... To love Him, the infinite, the omniscient One, with the whole strength, and mind, and heart, means the highest development of every power. It means that in the whole being—the body, the mind, as well as the soul—the image of God is to be restored."
p. 17: "It is the work of true education to develop this power, to train the youth to be thinkers, and not mere reflectors of other men's thought."
p. 18: "Higher than the highest human thought can reach is God's ideal for His children. Godliness—godlikeness—is the goal to be reached."

10. *I Corinthians 9:24-26 (NEB)*: "You know (do you not?) that at the sports all the runners run the race, though only one wins the prize. Like them, run to win! But every athlete goes into strict training. They do it to win a fading wreath; we, a wreath that never fades. For my part, I run with a clear goal before me; I am like a boxer who does not beat the air ..."

the senses—their eyes, their ears—are the gates which allow passage, or serve as guardians in the programming process, and determine to a large extent the subsequent ability to respond to the voice of God and their need and cries of their fellow men (11, 12).

For this reason, all types of information that clutter the storage capacity with erroneous concepts, false theories and principles, dangerous motives, unnecessary trivia, and unbalanced emphasis, must be shunned. Instead, the mind must be filled with the principles of truth and a knowledge of God.

Adventists recognize the reality of the world in which they live and the value of the statement made in Jesus' prayer to His father before His crucifixion, not that He take them out of the world but that He protect them from the evil (13).

They perceive their mission as a mission to the world. They understand it as a mission that can only be accomplished as they mingle with the world. So far as they behold the things of the world while serving their mission, they consent to accept the risks involved. Surely, they say, "Our Saviour did no less." But so far as it is possible, by the grace of God and the power of the Holy Spirit, without forfeiting their opportunities for proclaiming their God-given message, they endeavor to keep themselves unspotted by the world (14).

In this context, Adventists have discouraged attendance at most of the entertainments of the world. They have tended to shy away from those classics in literature and art that exalt the human and the satanic over the principles of God. They are aware of the power of music and have encouraged the pure forms. In all things they have taught and admonished the value of beholding the things of God.

Pride led to the downfall of Lucifer. Using that vice, he was successful in defeating Adam and Eve. It is undoubtedly the characteristic which most often interferes with a person's relationship with God and a sense of security in His dominion over them. Competitive sports, business practices, and whatever else caters to and encourages self-sufficiency and independence from God endangers one's salvation and interferes with the mission of the Advent Movement (15, 16, 17).

Adventists love beauty and thrill at the sight of the things that God has created in this world to enjoy. But they believe that jewelry, make-up, stylish clothing, and all similar types of "things" that tend to focus their attention upon themselves detract from the beauty of the living Christ within and the way He is perceived by the world He is trying to reach. As such, "things" are inappropriate decorations which clash with His simple beauty (18).

Wealth may be a blessing or a curse. In this world it may be a medium by which to enhance the cause of Christ or a tool in the hands of the devil with which to destroy. There is a principle in the universe that Adventists believe must control the use of their means if the spirit of Christ is indeed dwelling within them. This principle of benevolence is expressed throughout God's creation. "We receive that we may give." It is a principle based upon self-sacrificing love. It is often one of the most visible expressions depicting true allegiance (19, 20, 21).

Following the example of the ancient patriarchs and the subsequent Law of Moses, Adventists subscribe to the tithing system in giving (22, 23). They believe that ten percent of their increase belongs to the cause of God and is given to be used for the support of those who serve in the capacity of God's spokesmen as ministers, teachers, etc. They believe this system is equitable to both the poor and the rich and allows opportunities for all to experience the joy inherent in supporting the work of God.

In addition to the tithe, they believe that they are God's stewards and that all of their blessings are received to share with the world in need. The direction of the sharing is an individual direction under the control of the Holy Spirit and takes many forms and characteristics depending upon the person and the circumstances.

An interesting observation that has been made by Adventists is that God blesses their commitment to Him. And, because of that commitment, they believe that they are often given greater means and greater opportunities whereby to give once again. Thus, the principle of benevolence becomes an important characteristic of the Advent people serving to enhance the mission of the Movement in proclaiming God's love to the world.

Since they believe that their means beyond those necessary for their immediate needs are to be given for the blessing of the world in preparation for their

and everything thus illumined is all light. And so the hymn says: 'Awake, sleeper, rise from the dead, and Christ will shine upon you.' Be most careful then how you conduct yourselves; like sensible men, not like simpletons. Use the present opportunity to the full, for these are evil days. So do not be fools, but try to understand what the will of the Lord is. Do not give way to drunkenness and the dissipation that goes with it, but let the Holy Spirit fill you: speak to one another in psalms, hymns, and songs; sing and make music in your hearts to the Lord; and in the name of our Lord Jesus Christ give thanks every day for everything to our God and Father. Be subject to one another out of reverence for Christ."

15. I John 2:16 (NIV): "For everything in the world—the cravings of sinful man, the lust of his eyes, and the boasting of what he has and does—comes not from the father but from the world."

16. Matthew 18:4 (NEB): "Let a man humble himself till he is like this child, and he will be the greatest in the kingdom of Heaven."

17. Proverbs 29:23 (NIV): "A man's pride brings him low, but a man of lowly spirit gains honor."

18. I Peter 3:3-6 (NEB): "Your beauty should reside, not in outward adornment—the braiding of the hair, or jewelry, or dress—but in the inmost centre of your being, with its imperishable ornament, a gentle, quiet spirit, which is of high value in the sight of God. Thus it was among God's people in days of old: the women who fixed their hopes on him adorned themselves by submission to their husbands. Such was Sarah, who obeyed Abraham and called him, 'my master.' Her children you have now become, if you do good and show no fear."

19. James 5:3 (NIV):
"Your gold and silver are corroded. Their corrosion will testify against you and eat your flesh like fire. You have hoarded wealth in the last days."

20. II Corinthians 9:8, 11, 12 (NEB): "And it is in God's power to provide you richly with every good gift; thus you will have ample means in yourselves to meet each and every situation, with enough and to spare for every good cause . . . and you will always be rich enough to be generous. Through our action, such generosity will issue in thanksgiving to God, for as a piece of willing service this is not only a contribution toward the needs of God's people; more than that, it overflows in a flood of thanksgiving to God."

21. Matthew 6:19-21 (NEB): "Do not store up for yourselves treasure on earth, where it grows rusty and moth-eaten, and thieves break in to steal it. Store up treasure in heaven, where there is no moth and no rust to spoil it, no thieves to break in and steal. For where your treasure is, there will your heart be also."

22. Leviticus 27:30 (NIV): "A tithe of everything from the land, whether grain from the soil or fruit from the trees, belongs to the Lord; it is holy to the Lord."

23. Malachi 3:10 (NIV): "Bring the whole tithe into the storehouse, that there may be food in my house. Test me in this,' says the Lord Almighty, 'and see if I will not throw open the floodgates of heaven and pour out so much blessing that you will not have room enough for it."

Lord's return, they have developed a position of conservatism in regards to such things as investments, speculation, life insurance, retirement plans, etc.

Yes, Adventists claim to have reason for existence. But more than that, they have developed a system of response designed to reinforce that reason and to give them the resources needed to accomplish their mission. But the next question to pursue is this: Is the message that they claim the calling to bear a message of truth from a loving God and a true warning of certain destruction, or is it a message of fear designed to create further division among the churches of Jesus Christ? For, if it is anything other than what they claim, the designation of "cult" must certainly have validity. Before attempting to answer this question, and in order to better understand the answer, it is important to learn more about this people and the message they bear.

REFERENCE

White, Ellen G. Education. *Mountain View, CA: Pacific Press Publishing Association, 1952.*

Chapter II

A World Awakened, A People Born: The Beginnings of Adventism

October 8, 1844, dawned as any other autumn day in New England. There was one exception: in many fields and garden plots scattered around the countryside, the harvesting of crops was ignored by devout Christian believers of many faiths because they were convinced that this day would fulfill the anticipated return of their Lord and Savior, Jesus Christ. Before the dawning of another day, this hope would be seen as an obvious delusion and become recorded in history by the kindest of historians as the "Great Disappointment."

It happened this way:

On the evening before the Crucifixion, as Jesus and His disciples were gathered in the Upper Room, in Jerusalem, to celebrate the Passover supper, He told them that He would not again partake with them in this service until He would do so in His kingdom (1, 2).

Some forty or so days later, after His death and resursection, He was talking with them again on the Mount of Olives, just to the east of Jerusalem. He had appeared unto them several times previously, confirming the reality of His resurrection (3, 4). On this occasion, while He was speaking, He was suddenly lifted up from among them into the clouds of the sky. In His place there appeared two angels speaking to the disciples and telling them that, "This same Jesus which has been taken up from among you will so come in like manner as you have seen Him go into heaven" (Acts 1:11). In their frustration and grief following the crucifixion, the disciples were ripe for some good news. They took these words of the angels and absorbed them into their lives as a dry sponge absorbs water (5).

Not many days later with this hope in their hearts, while contemplating their new mission, the Holy Spirit was poured out upon them in a Pentecostal blessing. It filled them with power and drove them to proclaim their new-found hope to the ends of the world (6, 7).

They were convinced that the teachings of Jesus were true, that His death and resurrection were real events and that His own words and the angels' promise would soon be fulfilled: Jesus would indeed return to set up His kingdom which would be an everlasting Kingdom (8).

1. *Luke 22:17, 18 (NEB):* "Then he took a cup, and after giving thanks he said, 'Take this and share it among yourselves; for I tell you, from this moment I shall drink from the fruit of the vine no more until the time when the kingdom of God comes.'"

2. *John 14:1-3 (King James Version):* "Let not your heart be troubled: ye believe in God, believe also in me. In my Father's house are many mansions: if it were not so, I would have told you. I go to prepare a place for you. And if I go and prepare a place for you, I will come again, and receive you unto myself; that where I am, there ye may be also."

3. *Acts 1:3 (NEB):* "He showed himself to these men after his death, and gave ample proof that he was alive: over a period of forty days, he appeared to them and taught them about the kingdom of God."

4. *Acts 1:9, 10 (NEB):* "When he had said this, as they watched, he was lifted up, and a cloud removed him from their sight. As he was going, and as they were gazing intently into the sky, all at once there stood beside them two men in white who said , 'Men of Galilee, why stand there looking up into the sky?'"

5. *Luke 24:51-53 (NIV):* "While he was blessing them, he left them and was taken up into heaven. Then they worshipped him and returned to Jerusalem with great joy. And they stayed continually at the temple, praising God."

6. *Acts 2:4 (NEB): "And they were all filled with the Holy Spirit and began to talk in other tongues, as the Spirit gave them power of utterance."*

7. *Acts 3:20, 21 (NEB): "Then the Lord may grant you a time of recovery and send you the Messiah he has already appointed, that is, Jesus. He must be received into heaven until the time of universal restoration comes, of which God spoke by his holy prophets."*

8. *Daniel 2:44 (NEB): "In the period of those kings the God of heaven will establish a kingdom which shall never be destroyed; that kingdom shall never pass to another people; it shall shatter and make an end of all these kingdoms, while it shall itself endure forever."*

9. *Colossians 1:23 (NEB): "Only you must continue in your faith, firm on your foundations, never to be dislodged from the hope offered in the gospel which you heard. This is the gospel which has been proclaimed in the whole creation under heaven; and I, Paul, have become its minister."*

10. *Revelation 6:12, 13 (NEB): "Then I watched as he broke the sixth seal. And there was a violent earthquake; the sun turned black as a funeral pall and the moon all red as blood; the stars in the sky fell to the earth, like figs shaken down by a gale."*

11. *Matthew 24:29 (NEB): "As soon as the distress of those days has passed, the sun will be darkened, the moon will not give her light, the stars will fall from the sky, the celestial powers will be shaken."*

12. *Joel 2:31 (NEB): "The sun shall be turned into darkness and the moon into blood before the great and terrible day of the Lord comes."*

Although the disciples in the early church anticipated an early fulfillment of the promised return, and although the Gospel went to the whole world in that first generation in seeming fulfillment of the necessary prerequisites (9), Jesus did not return during their generation, nor during the next, or the next. In fact, quite early in the Christian church, in the struggle over orthodoxy and survival, the Promise gradually lost urgency and was soon nearly forgotten altogether.

As one studies the history of the church in the intervening centuries, there is only occasional mention of the early return of Jesus. In most instances where it is referred to, it is generally viewed as an event to occur at some distant future point. Then, quite dramatically, several events transpired in the eighteenth century that began to impact upon human thought. A great earthquake centered in Lisbon, Portugal, on November 1, 1755, set the stage for people to return to the Scriptures in study of the signs that were to precede the return of the Lord.

Later in that same century, an event occurred in the eastern United States that seemed to fulfill other pre-Advent prophecies described by the prophet Joel in the Old Testament and by Jesus and John in the New Testament.

On May 19, 1780, the skies became overcast by a thick gloom that settled upon the land. By noon it had become so dense that the chickens flew to their roosts, and the cows came home to be milked. Candles were lit in homes and legislative halls. A sense of doom pervaded the whole countryside. That night the full moon rose in the eastern sky, red as blood.

Until now, the cause of that darkness has not been satisfactorily explained. Whether it was caused by a supernatural means or by some kind of natural phenomenon, its effects were the same. People recognized it as prophecy fulfilled and began to focus their thoughts on the return of our Lord.

Some time passed. People searched the Scriptures. Then, on November 13, 1833, the greatest star shower of all time illumined the nighttime sky. It was as if the whole sky was filled with fireworks at once. And again the world was forced to consider their times (10, 11, 12).

But it was not only the signs in the heavens that drew men to search the Scriptures. Many students of the Bible recognized the events surrounding the French Revolution as further evidence that the time of the end was at hand. The glorification of atheism, the legislation opposing the Bible, and the exiling of Pope Pius VI in 1798 all indicated the fulfillment of Daniel's prophecy (Daniel 12:7) and the end of the all things (Maxwell, 1981, 277, 280-292).

Undoubtedly stimulated by the thinking of the times, a young man by the name of William Miller, a farmer turned politician from New England, struggled with the many variant religious philosophies of his time. He arrived at a point in his personal convictions where he felt that he must find out for himself whether or not there was any truth to the written word of God in the Holy Scriptures. In his search to satisfy his curiosity, he delved deeply into the Scriptures, utilizing cross references, concordances, and all available means to compare Scripture with Scripture.

In the course of this study, he became convinced, not only of the validity of the Holy Book and the God which it promoted, but that Jesus would return again. More than this, according to his discoveries, Jesus was due to return soon.

Studying the prophecies of Daniel, Chapters 8 and 9 (13, 14), William Miller arrived at the date of 1844 for the return of Jesus (13). By interpreting the prophecy regarding the cleansing of the sanctuary in Daniel 8:14 as the purification of this world by fire, he concluded that it must also refer to the Second Coming of Christ.

Armed with this conviction, he could not contain the spirit within himself (15, 16). He soon took up preaching and proclaimed his convictions far and wide. Miller was an educated man, a man of respect in his community, and one who was quite conservative in his willingness to depart from traditional thinking. However, the power of his convictions regarding the Second Coming overpowered his reservations (17).

When on that October day in 1844 Jesus failed to return, Miller and his followers were understandably greatly disappointed as well as terribly embarrassed (18). Although Miller subsequently faded into the background, his contribution had been made and God's purpose accomplished. The world had been awakened in preparation for its final call. In his stead, some of his followers went back to the Scriptures in an attempt to discover where they had gone wrong (19, 20).

Out of this study grew a movement whose proponents clung to the belief that Jesus would indeed soon return. (Other aspects of their research will be

13. Daniel 9:25-27 (KJV): "Know therefore and understand, that from the going forth of the commandment to restore and to build Jerusalem unto the Messiah the Prince shall be seven weeks, and threescore and two weeks: the street shall be built again, and the wall, even in troublous times. And after threescore and two weeks shall Messiah be cut off, but not for himself: and the people of the prince that shall come shall destroy the city and the sanctuary; and the end thereof shall be with a flood, and unto the end of the war desolations are determined. And he shall confirm the convenant with many for one week: and in the midst of the week he shall cause the sacrifice and the obligation to cease, and for the overspreading of abominations he shall make it desolate, even until the consummation, and that determined shall be poured upon the desolate."

14. Daniel 8:14 (KJV): "And he said unto me, Unto two thousand and three hundred days, then shall the sanctuary be cleansed."

15. Acts 4:7, 8 (NEB): "They brought the apostles before the court and began the examination. 'By what power,' they asked, 'or by what name have such men as you done this?' Then Peter, filled with the Holy Spirit, answered, . . ."

16. Luke 21:15 (NEB): ". . . because I myself will give you power of utterance and a wisdom which no opponent will be able to resist or refute."

17. Acts 4:20 (NEB): "We cannot possibly give up speaking of things we have seen and heard."

18. Revelation 10:8-11 (NEB): "Then the voice which I heard from heaven was speaking to me again, and it said, 'Go and take the open scroll in the hand of the angel that stands on the sea and the land.' So I went to the angel and asked him to give me the little scroll.

He said to me, 'Take it, and eat it. It will turn your stomach sour, although in your mouth it will taste sweet as honey.' So I took the little scroll from the angel's hand and ate it, and in my mouth it did taste sweet as honey; but when I swallowed it, my stomach turned sour. Then they said to me, 'Once again you must utter prophecies over peoples and nations and languages and many kings.'"

19. Acts 17:11 (NEB): "On arrival they made their way to the synagogue. The Jews here were more civil than those at Thessalonica: they received the message with great eagerness, studying the scriptures every day to see whether it was as they said."

20. Romans 15:4 (NEB): "For all the ancient scriptures were written for our own instruction, in order that through the encouragement they give us we may maintain our hope with fortitude."

discussed in subsequent chapters.) From this beginning, traumatic as it seems even in retrospect, the concept of the Second Coming of Christ as a reality was tossed into the limelight and became the focus of emphasis around which all other doctrines of the emerging Seventh-day Adventist church grew. It is this "Advent Movement" as the believers referred to themselves that has through the intervening years faithfully fulfilled their witness throughout the world. Today, the Second Coming of Christ and the end of the world are beliefs accepted by many people of many faiths in all lands. It is impossible even in retrospect to determine the extent of influence that the Seventh-day Adventist Church has had in helping to bring world religious thought to this point. Certainly, it has not been the only instrument which God has used to accomplish this purpose. Still, one could seriously suggest that had it not been for the worldwide impact of Seventh-day Adventists, the doctrine of the Second Coming of Jesus would not even now be so widely accepted and understood.

One question comes to mind: Would God use a small religious cult to accomplish His purposes? Put in other words, would God use evil that good may come?

Of course, there are other possible explanations that might account for the association of Seventh-day Adventists with the Second Coming of Jesus. Perhaps the events and their consequences were purely coincidental and in no way related to the leading of God. Certainly, much more information will be necessary before that determination can be made.

Closely related to the doctrine of the soon return of Jesus that helped to establish Adventism upon a firm foundation was an understanding of the concept of the warfare that is being waged between the forces of good and evil behind the scenes of human view. Major portions of this truth had previously been gleaned from Scripture by earlier Christians and served well to help explain many of the difficult questions people ask about a loving God in an evil world. We will examine this warfare in the next chapter.

REFERENCE

Maxwell, C. Mervyn. God Cares. Vol. 2. Boise, ID: Pacific Press Publishing Association, 1981.

Chapter III

The War to End All Wars:
The Battle Between Good and Evil

Adventists envision themselves as messengers commissioned to bear God's last warning message to an erring world, a world bent on a path of self-destruction. Adventists sometimes refer to the special message with which they believe they have been entrusted as "The Elijah Message." Like Elijah of Old Testament times, and John the Baptist in the days of Jesus, Adventists believe that they are called to prepare the world for the return of Christ. They also refer to themselves as the "remnant," a term suggesting the last generation of the true followers of God. The message that they feel commissioned to proclaim is referred to as "the everlasting gospel" which is understood to be the "Good News" (Gospel) as it applies to our day and generation. This "Good News" has been variously referred to as "The Truth," "Present Truth," "The Third Angel's Message," and "Righteousness by Faith." These references are the basis upon which the designation of Adventism as a "cult" is most often made. Is the designation justified?

In order to be able to begin to understand the significance of these terms and to place the teachings related to them in proper perspective, it is first necessary to see a picture of the Adventist understanding of what sin is, how it began and developed, what it has done and is doing in the world and in the universe at large, and how the problem of sin will ultimately be resolved. This process of resolving the sin problem is described as warfare between God and the forces of good, and Satan and the agencies of evil. It is often referred to as "The Great Controversy."

Eons before this world existed there was God and the universe He had created that was composed of billions and billions of galaxies and stars. Somewhere among that vast expanse of space was God and His dwelling place that we now call heaven. Inhabiting many of the planets encircling the innumerable stars were intelligent beings enjoying the gift of life. In heaven itself angels beyond count experienced the joy of life and ministry. Everywhere throughout the universe was harmony and peace. Indeed, the inhabitants were not

1. Ezekiel 28:14, 15 (NEB): "I set you with a towering cherub as guardian; you were on God's holy hill and you walked proudly among stones that flashed with fire. You were blameless in all your ways from the day of your birth until your iniquity came to light."

2. Isaiah 14:12-14 (NEB): "How you have fallen from heaven, bright morning star, felled to the earth, sprawling helpless across the nations. You thought in your own mind, I will scale the heavens; I will set my throne high above the stars of God, I will sit on the mountain where the gods meet in the far recesses of the north. I will rise high above the cloudbanks and make myself like the Most High."

3. Revelation 12:7 (NEB): "Then war broke out in heaven. Michael and his angels waged war upon the dragon."

4. Revelation 12:9 (NEB): "So the great dragon was thrown down, that serpent of old that led the whole world astray, whose name is Satan, or the Devil—thrown down to the earth, and his angels with him."

5. Genesis 1:27, 28 (NEB): "So God created man in his own image; in the image of God he created him; male and female he created them. God blessed them and said to them, 'Be fruitful and increase, fill the earth and subdue it, rule over the fish in the sea, the birds of heaven, and every living thing that moves upon the earth.'"

6. Genesis 2:8 (NEB): "Then the Lord God planted a garden in Eden away to the east, and there he put the man whom he had formed."

7. Genesis 2:9, 17 (NEB): "The Lord God made trees spring from the ground, all trees pleasant to look at and good for food; and in the middle of the garden he set the tree of life and the tree of the knowledge of good and evil. . . but you must not

even conscious that anything else existed—until one day things began to change. (The Biblical record does not reveal when in the course of time this happened, neither does it give an explanation or excuse for what was occurring.) An angel of the very highest order, Lucifer by name, the most beautiful and exalted in all of heaven, developed jealousy and a thirst for God's throne in his heart (1, 2). (Many Adventists believe that the whole problem started when Lucifer discovered that he was not a member of the planning committee preparing for the creation of planet Earth.) As it turned out, what appeared first as a bit of inflated self-importance rapidly turned to outright rebellion and all-out war (3). Aided by Lucifer's prestige and position, the rebellion spread throughout the realm of heaven among its many hosts. Word of the uprising also reached faraway worlds, and questions were raised as to the purpose and authority of God in all of this commotion. The peace and unity of heaven was turned topsy-turvy, and in its place developed fear and distrust for one another and for God Himself—for maybe the accusations were really true after all!?

True to the nature of love, for God is love, Lucifer and his co-conspirators were approached from every conceivable angle in an effort to win them back to the unity of heaven (I John 4:8). Although some efforts resulted in brief changes, the problem persisted and grew. Eventually, in order to preserve the very existence of heaven and to protect the unwary, God found it necessary to exclude Lucifer from heaven once and for all. With him went one third of the hosts of angels (4).

In the course of time, according to the book of Genesis, the earth was created. As the crowning act of that creation, God created two human beings in His own image and placed them in a garden home in which to live (5, 6). They were given dominion over the whole world and admonished to multiply and fill the earth to rule over it. Like all other created beings before them, they were designed with the capacity to live forever in a world perfectly designed to meet their every need.

In the center of their garden home, God placed two special trees, the tree of life and the tree of the knowledge of good and evil (7). Adam and Eve were instructed that the garden and all of its bounties were there for them to enjoy with one exception: the fruit of one of the trees at the middle, the tree of the knowledge of good and evil, was not to be eaten or even touched lest they die. This tree was designed by God to be the pledge of their obedience to Him. It was a test of their loyalty, that if proven, would assure their perpetual life and provide freedom from Satan's attempts to lead them to join him in rebellion. Only at the tree would Satan have access to tempt them. They were not ignorant of this fact, for God had forewarned them of Satan's plight and his certain attacks upon them.

Quite contrary to God's warning, Eve found herself one day beside the forbidden tree. Looking up she saw a beautiful flying serpent among the branches. Suddenly, it appeared that the serpent was talking to her. "Eve, did God say that you may not eat of the fruit of this tree?" To her affirmative response, the voice again spoke, "You will not die, God knows that when you eat of it, your eyes will be opened and you will be like God knowing good from evil" (Genesis 3:4, 5).

Eve was caught by Satan's deception. She had disobeyed and now Satan had trapped her. Yet, she was not aware of her plight. The fruit was good to eat, and pleasant to taste. Quickly, she ran to Adam with her "newly discovered" experience and enticed him to taste and see for himself. Anxious to please her, he, too, ate of the fruit and joined her in disobedience and disloyalty (8).

That which at first seemed to Eve to be exhilarating very rapidly lost its enchantment when Adam and she became aware of the fact that they were now naked and lacking the divine glory that had previously surrounded them (9). With this, fear began to mount in their minds. As the time for the evening visit with God came around they found themselves hiding from His presence instead of joyously anticipating His arrival as on previous occasions.

One can imagine the turmoil which was going on in their minds during this time, wondering how God would react to their deed, while at the same time continuing to question the truthfulness of His statement telling them that they would die if they ate of the tree. Obviously, they were both still very much alive.

When the Lord did come to the garden, it was only very reluctantly that they responded to His call. Adam's first response to God was one of blame for giving him such a woman. After all, she had been the cause for leading him into trouble. Likewise, Eve failed to acknowledge her wrongdoing and blamed the serpent (10).

eat from the tree of the knowledge of good and evil, for when you eat of it you will surely die."

8. Genesis 3:4-6 (NEB): "The serpent said, 'Of course you will not die. God knows that as soon as you eat it, your eyes will be opened and you will be like gods knowing both good and evil.' When the woman saw that the fruit of the tree was good to eat, and that it was pleasing to the eye and tempting to contemplate, she took some and ate it. She also gave her husband some and he ate it."

9. Genesis 3:7-10 (NEB): "Then the eyes of both of them were opened and they discovered that they were naked; so they stitched fig-leaves together and made themselves loin cloths. The man and his wife heard the sound of the Lord God walking in the garden at the time of the evening breeze and hid from the Lord God among the trees of the garden. But the Lord God called to the man and said to him, 'Where are you?' He replied, 'I heard the sound as you were walking in the garden, and I was afraid because I was naked, and I hid myself.'"

10. Genesis 3:12, 13 (NEB): "The man said, 'The woman you gave me for a companion, she gave me fruit from the tree and I ate it.' Then the Lord God said to the woman, 'What is this that you have done?' The woman said, 'The serpent tricked me, and I ate.'"

11. Romans 6:16 (NEB): "You know well enough that if you put yourselves at the disposal of a master, to obey him, you are slaves of the master whom you obey; and this is true whether you serve sin, with death as its result; or obedience, with righteousness as its result."

12. II Peter 2:19 (NEB): "They promise them freedom, but are themselves slaves of corruption; for a man is the slave of whatever has mastered him."

13. Romans 5:12 (NEB): "Mark what follows. It was through one man that sin entered the world, and through sin death, and thus death pervaded the whole human race, inasmuch as all men have sinned."

14. Romans 7:19 (NEB): "The good which I want to do, I fail to do; but what I do is the wrong which is against my will."

15. I Peter 5:8 (KJV): "Be sober, be vigilant; because your adversary the devil, as a roaring lion, walketh about, seeking whom he may devour."

16. Romans 6:23 (NEB): "For sin pays a wage, and the wage is death, but God gives freely, and his gift is eternal life, in union with Christ Jesus our Lord."

17. Ephesians 1:9, 10 (NEB): ". . . such was his will and pleasure determined beforehand in Christ—to be put into effect when the time was ripe; namely, that the universe, all in heaven and on earth, might be brought into unity in Christ."

18. Colossians 1:20 (NEB): "Through Him God chose to reconcile the whole universe to Himself, making peace through the shedding of His blood upon the cross—to reconcile all things, whether on earth or in heaven, through Him alone."

The record is short, but within these few paragraphs, it is possible to develop a fairly concise picture of what occurred when our ancestors yielded the domain of their new kingdom to the serpent (11, 12). There was guilt. There was fear. There was anger. There was resentment.

The changes which they had so recently undergone as their eyes were opened to the knowledge of evil gained by their experience that day would be passed on to all future generations (13, 14). From that point on, human nature would not be the same but would share in the knowledge of evil and be inclined toward it. Further, Satan, their conqueror, would be free to follow them everywhere in order to hound them with his temptations (15). But God, being the personification of love, could not and would not allow destruction of His creatures without applying every possible means of intervention (16 through 20).

As is true of all of love's activities, any intervention must occur only in the context of perfect freedom. Coercion and force would have no role in bringing the lost race back to Him. But even more than reconciling the human race was at stake. Rebellion had originated in heaven with Satan. Angels and intelligent beings throughout heaven and the universe had heard Satan's arguments against the value and veracity of God's way of governing His universe. They had listened to His arguments that although God spoke of love and the freedom of every individual, in effect there was no real love or freedom, and all individuals were subject to God who Himself, it was alleged, played by other rules.

The plan for restoration must once and for all squelch the doubt and questions raised by Satan. And it must offer the opportunity for complete restoration of any of those who had fallen and become subject to death. Sin and rebellion must be dealt with in such a way that the earth and the whole universe would be secured from any repeat experience (21). This was the need that presented itself to God when Adam and Eve partook of the fruit of the tree.

As God ushered Adam and Eve from the Garden, He shared with them those aspects of the plan of restoration which they could comprehend. The details are not all recorded. Eve was told that henceforth she would bear children with pain and sorrow, and she would be subject to her husband (Genesis 3:16). Adam was told that the ground would be cursed for his sake, somehow indicating that even the hard experiences of this life have a purpose in restoration (Genesis 3:17-19).

Together they were given the promise that restoration would be provided as God Himself would come into this world, born of a virgin, to pay the price for their sin. They would die and return to the dust from which they had come as a result of their sin. But through the Promised One there would be opportunity for a recreation, a restoration to their original state, once again in harmony with God and the universe around them.

But to accomplish this, the God-child who would come must die (22). This had to be so not only to satisfy the legal claims brought on by sin, but to convince the world regarding the nature of God's love and the extent to which true love will go in ministering to the needs of one in need. Nothing less than self-sacrificing love could meet this objective (23 through 30).

In order to remind Adam and Eve and subsequent generations of this promise, they were instructed to sacrifice a lamb (or other animal as indicated) in acknowledgment of their sin and as a symbol of both their repentance and their faith in the promised Messiah to come.

Then, those who believed in Him would again have the chance to enjoy eternal life. For the Bible is clear: "He is patient with you, not wanting anyone to perish, but everyone to come to righteousness." (II Peter 3:9, NIV).

The Bible is not the only source of evidence for the Messiah. In nearly every ancient culture and religion one finds symbols depicting a mother and child. Often the child is depicted as a God-figure and many times has been the object of worship.

Likewise, the concept of sacrifices exists in nearly every ancient religion and persists to this day in some. It is true that the full significance of the sacrificial system has been lost; but its form persists. Both of these are very definite indicators that the plan of God was made plain to the early inhabitants of this planet from the beginning. Perhaps even more interesting is the recently rediscovered evidence that the whole plan of redemption was told in the patterns of the stars and constellations, dating back to the most ancient time (Seiss, 1977, 12-14).

There is a prophecy recorded in the third chapter of Genesis, verse 15, which has for ages been considered a

19. *John 3:16 (NEB):* "God loved the world so much that He gave His only Son, that everyone who has faith in Him may not die but have eternal life."

20. *I Timothy 2:4 (NEB):* ". . . approved by God our Saviour, whose will it is that all men should find salvation and come to know the truth."

21. *Nahum 1:9 (NIV):* "Whatever they plot against the Lord he will bring to an end; trouble will not come a second time."

22. *Genesis 3:15 (NEB):* "I will put enmity between you and the woman, between your brood and hers. They shall strike at your head, and you shall strike at their heel."

23. *Isaiah 53:5 (NEB):* ". . . but he was pierced for our transgressions, tortured for our iniquities; the chastisement he bore is health for us and by his scourging we are healed."

24. *Galatians 3:13 (NEB):* "Christ bought us freedom from the curse of the law by becoming for our sake an accursed thing; for Scripture says, 'A curse is on everyone who is hanged on a gibbet.'"

25. *I Peter 3:18 (NEB):* "For Christ also died for our sins once and for all. He, the just, suffered for the unjust, to bring us to God."

26. *I Peter 1:19 (NEB):* "The price was paid in precious blood, as it were of a lamb without mark or blemish—the blood of Christ."

27. *II Timothy 1:9, 10 (NEB):* "It is he who brought us salvation and called us to a dedicated life, not for any merit of ours but of his own purpose and his own grace, which was granted to us in Christ Jesus from all eternity, but has now at length been brought fully into view by the appearance on earth of our Saviour Jesus Christ. For he has broken the power of death and brought life

prophecy foretelling the messiah (31). This prophecy of promise appears in the record of God’s statement of curse to the serpent who had been responsible for tempting Eve. The serpent was told that he would injure the foot or heel of the woman’s offspring including the messiah, but that this same messiah would deal a mortal blow to the serpent’s head.

This prophecy along with other indicators that have already been cited identified a conflict that would occur between good and evil in this world, that would eventually defeat evil and vindicate good. And while human beings, blinded to the reality of the unseen, struggle to find meaning in the difficult experiences of this life, the battle for their loyalties continues behind the scenes (32 through 34). God wages war with the only weapons that He knows, wielded in love: weapons of patience, long-suffering, justice, and mercy. The enemy battles with an arsenal of deception and destruction. Satan’s only constraints are the constraints wrought by the natural consequences of his evil devisings. Seventh-day Adventists believe that the conflict is real and is fought by real and intelligent beings, although invisible to human eyes. They believe that Jesus Christ is the seed of promise, and by His sacrifice on the Roman cross satisfied all the requirements for the restoration of those who accept the gift. And they believe that Satan is the dragon and the fallen angels his accomplices. They are real, living, intelligent, and cunning beings actively engaged in efforts to limit or prevent the effects of God’s grace on the human heart and mind.

Furthermore, in these last days of the earth’s history, more than ever before Satan is as a roaring lion seeking those whom he may devour (I Peter 5:8). The conflict for the human mind is intense for the stakes are high. But the nature of true love will be vindicated, and God’s authority and right to rule the universe will be acknowledged forever. This will be the last experience with sin that the universe will ever experience. For this reason, God has had to allow sin to run its full, though heart-rending, course for six thousand long and painful years. For every intelligent being must be convinced in his own mind so indelibly that alternative behaviors will not again be considered. This has been an overview of the Adventist concept of the warfare between good and evil. Later chapters will fill in many details as they apply to end-time events and the purpose and role of Adventism in those events.

REFERENCE

Seiss, Joseph A. Gospel in the Stars. *Grand Rapids, MI: Kregel Publications, 1977.*

Chapter IV

The Judgment

1. I John 4:18 (NEB): "There is no room for fear in love; perfect love banishes fear. For fear brings with it the pains of judgment, and anyone who is afraid has not attained to love in its perfection."

2. Hebrews 2:14, 15 (NEB): "The children of a family share the same flesh and blood, and so he too shared ours, so that through death he might break the power of him who had death at his command, that is, the devil; and might liberate those who, through fear of death, had all their lifetime been in servitude."

3. I John 4:9 (NEB): "For God is love; and his love was disclosed to us in this, that he sent his only Son into the world to bring us life."

4. Genesis 3:4, 5 (NEB): "The serpent said, 'Of course you will not die. God knows that as soon as you eat it, your eyes will be opened and you will be like gods knowing both good and evil.'"

5. Revelation 12:9 (NEB): "So the great dragon was thrown down, that serpent of old that led the whole world astray, whose name is Satan, or the Devil—thrown down to the earth, and his angels with him."

6. John 8:44 (NEB): "Your father is the devil and you choose to carry out your father's desires. He was a murderer from the beginning, and is not rooted in the truth; there is no truth in him. When he tells a lie, he is speaking his own language, for he is a liar and the father of lies."

Satan has been all too successful in convincing the human race that God's claim of love is a farce and His pattern of justice naive. There are probably no issues discussed in religious circles that trigger more negative emotion than the issues of reward and punishment (heaven and hell). In many religions the Supreme God is the one who rewards the good; He is also the one who wreaks His vengeance upon those who dare to defy Him.

The punishment of the wicked has been billed throughout history as a fearful act of a vengeful God. This has struck paralyzing fear even into the hearts of Christians. In fact, Christians have undoubtedly superseded all other religious peoples in portraying the punishment of the wicked by their descriptions of the eternal fires of Hell.

Such teaching has done two things: It has created confusion and anger in the minds of those who cannot reconcile an infinitely loving God with the everlasting torment so often described as the punishment of the wicked. To them it does not make sense that for seventy years of life on this earth (no matter how badly lived), there may be billions of years searing in the flames of hell as the "just reward." As a consequence, many reject God completely while others give Him lip service only.

The other effect is witnessed in those who serve God out of fear rather than from love. The direct consequence of such a motive for behavior is seen in the power which the "church" has exercised over the masses through the centuries.

Adventists believe that the holy record amply demonstrates the true nature of God as being infinitely loving (1). Furthermore, they believe that in the context of the battle between good and evil, Satan through his cunning deceptions is responsible for the characterization of God in such repulsive terms. It was Satan who lied to Adam and Eve when he told them they would not die by eating the fruit. And Adventists believe that it is his lies that continue to misrepresent God (2 through 6).

It is true that the Bible speaks often of God's wrath

and vengeance and appears to portray Him as insensitive and, at times, vindictive (7). Were it not for the overwhelming evidence throughout Scripture that God is a God of love and that His purpose and plan is one of reconciliation and restoration of the race rather than punishment, Adventists might have a difficult time defending their position in departing from a strictly traditional interpretation of Scripture regarding God's vengeance and wrath (8). For this departure, Adventists have been considered inconsistent in dealing with the Holy Word.

Such accusations may have merit for the critic accustomed to defending his religion by individual proof texts. Adventists believe that it has little merit, however, when viewed from the perspective of the Bible as a whole and what it is attempting to tell people about God.

The controversy between good and evil is, in essence, rooted in the accusation by the enemy that God's acts are unjust. Adventists do not believe this to be so. In fact, they believe that the various Biblical references to judgment are God's answer to His accusers.

It will be the judgment that ultimately vindicates the character of God and reestablishes His unquestioned sovereignty (9). It is also the judgment that determines those who are God's true followers (10) . And it is the judgment that deals with the element of rebellion that originated in Satan and his sympathizers both in heaven and on earth during the last six thousand years (11, 12). It is this that will expose the sin problem for what it really is and will assure that the problem will never again arise in the universe (Nahum 1:9 and Revelation 18:21).

The modern day judgment scene may be used as an example to help illustrate the process of God's judgment.

Before a judgment can be made there must be an accusation. The plaintiff must believe himself to have been wronged by another, the defendant. Each then, in an effort to realize every possible advantage of the law, contracts with an advocate (or attorney) to represent them before a court that generally consists of a judge and a jury.

Upon sensing wrongdoing or injury, the plaintiff contacts his attorney. After a brief evaluation as to the merits of the case, he files a grievance with the court. The court then delivers this grievance to the defend-

7. *Revelation 14:10, 11 (NEB):* "Whoever worships the beast and its image and receives its mark on his forehead or hand, he shall drink the wine of God's wrath, poured undiluted into the cup of his vengeance. He shall be tormented in sulphurous flames before the holy angels and before the Lamb. The smoke of their torment will rise forever and ever, and there will be no respite day or night for those who worship the beast and its image or receive the mark of its name."

8. *II Corinthians 5:18 (NEB):* "From first to last this has been the work of God. He has reconciled us men to himself through Christ, and he has enlisted us in this service of reconciliation."

9. *Romans 3:4 (NEB):* "God must be true though every man living were a liar; for we read in Scripture, 'When thou speakest thou shalt be vindicated, and win the verdict when thou are on trial.'"

10. *Psalms 58:11 (NEB):* "There is after all a reward for the righteous; after all, there is a God that judges on earth."

11. *Revelation 15:4 (NEB):* "Who shall not revere thee, Lord, and do homage to thy name? For thou alone art holy. All nations shall come and worship in thy presence, for thy just dealings stand revealed."

12. *Hebrews 4:12, 13 (NEB):* "For the word of God is alive and active. It cuts more keenly than any two-edged sword, piercing as far as the place where life and spirit, joints and marrow, divide. It sifts the purposes and thoughts of the heart. There is nothing in creation that can hide from Him, everything lies naked and exposed to the eyes of the One with whom we have to recon."

ant, who contacts his representing attorney to prepare his defense.

Then begins a period of investigation during which each party gathers evidence upon which to build his case. After some appropriate interval, the judge schedules a time for the court to sit. On the designated day, the defendant and his representing counsel meet the plaintiff and his counsel in the judgment hall before the judge and the accompanying jury.

Interested members of the public are often allowed to witness the proceedings. When all is in order, the gavel sounds and the trial begins. The counsels for the plaintiff and the defense present their respective arguments. The plaintiff and the defendant respond under oath to the interrogation of the opposing counsel, and witnesses are called who may add to the testimony of either.

When the evidence has been heard and summarized, the judge instructs the jury as to the nature of their responsibility, following which they go into seclusion to weigh the evidence and arrive at a judgment or decision in favor of either the plaintiff or the defendant. If the defendant is found guilty, his penalty must be determined by the judge or the jury and his sentence subsequently executed (placed in effect).

If, on the other hand, the jury finds in favor of the defense, the plaintiff is left with his alleged injury.

The judgment scene as described in Scripture depicts many of these same features. Satan (the plaintiff), described in the Bible as the accuser of the brethren, has filed his grievance (13 through 15). In it he states that all human beings are guilty of sin and deserve to die. They, as children of Adam and Eve, lost their royal status along with Adam and Eve and became Satan's subjects and fellow agents of rebellion against the laws of God. They were, therefore, subject to the same death sentence that God had pronounced against Satan.

In this grievance is an implied accusation against God as well for His part in rescuing His people and apparently acting contrary to his original warning statement that the wages of sin is death.

God is the judge who presides over the court (16). The jury consists of the intelligent beings throughout the universe (17, 18). The witnesses represent the members of the human race who have accepted God's offer for restoration.

13. *Revelation 12:10 (NEB): "Then I heard a voice in heaven proclaiming aloud: 'This is the hour of victory for our God, the hour of his sovereignty and power, when his Christ comes to his rightful rule. For the accuser of our brothers is overthrown, who day and night accused them before our God.'"*

14. *Zechariah 3:1 (NEB): "Then he showed me Joshua the high priest standing before the angel of the Lord, with the Adversary standing at his right hand to accuse him."*

15. *Jude 9 (NEB): "In contrast, when the archangel Michael was in debate with the devil, disputing the possession of Moses' body, he did not presume to condemn him in insulting words, but said, 'May the Lord rebuke you!'"*

16. *Psalms 50:6 (NEB): "The heavens proclaim his justice, for God himself is the judge."*

17. *Ephesians 1:10 (NEB): ". . . such was his will and pleasure determined beforehand in Christ—to be put into effect when the time was ripe: namely, that the universe, all in heaven and on earth, might be brought into a unity in Christ."*

18. *I Corinthians 4:9 (NEB): "For it seems to me God has made us apostles the most abject of mankind. We are like men condemned to death in the arena, a spectacle to the whole universe—angels as well as men."*

19. Romans 8:34 (NEB): "It is Christ—Christ who died, and more than that, was raised from the dead—is at God's right hand, and indeed pleads our cause."

20. Revelation 12:10 (NEB): "Then I heard a voice in heaven proclaiming aloud: 'This is the hour of victory for our God, the hour of his sovereignty and power, when his Christ comes to his rightful rule. For the accuser of our brothers is overthrown, who day and night accused them before our God."

21. Romans 14:11 (NEB): "For Scripture says, 'As I live, says the Lord, to me every knee shall bow and every tongue acknowledge God.'"

22. Romans 6:23 (NEB): "For sin pays a wage, and the wage is death, but God gives freely, and his gift is eternal life, in union with Christ Jesus our Lord."

23. Hebrews 9:9 (NEB): "All this is symbolic, pointing to the present time. The offerings and sacrifices there prescribed cannot give the worshipper inward perfection."

24. Hebrews 10:11, 12 (NEB): "Every priest stands performing his service daily and offering time after time the same sacrifices, which can never remove sins. But Christ offered for all time one sacrifice for sins, and took his seat at the right hand of God, where he waits henceforth until his enemies are made his footstool."

25. Leviticus 4:29, 30 (NEB): "He shall lay his hand on the head of the victim and slaughter it in the place where the whole-offering is slaughtered. The priest shall then take some of its blood with his finger and put it on the horns of the altar of whole-offering. All the rest of the blood he shall pour at the base of the altar."

Satan represents himself as plaintiff. The counsel for the defense is the crucified and risen Son of God (19). The Bible describes the outcome of the trial in favor of those who have accepted God's gift of redemptive restoration and vindicates God as fully just and worthy of His acclaimed authority as King of Kings and Lord of Lords (20). The plaintiff and his subjects (both angels and men), although unrepentant, join the rest of the universe on bended knee in acknowledgment of God's everlasting love and right to reign (21).

At this point the awful consequence of sin has been fully revealed, its secrets unmasked. There will no longer be purpose for life among the rebellious ones. The consequence of sin (i.e., death) means destruction for all who have not accepted God's divine plan (22).

This judgment scene was portrayed in symbols in the services of the ancient Hebrew sanctuary system (23). The many roles of Jesus, the Lamb of God, were depicted in the various ceremonies of this service.

When a person sinned, either knowingly or ignorantly, he brought a lamb or some other prescribed animal to the court of the synagogue. Here, by his own hand, he killed the animal in acknowledgment of his sin. The blood was then taken by the priest into the first of two apartments in the sanctuary and sprinkled upon the altar, symbolizing a transfer of the man's sin through the priest to the sanctuary. This service was performed over and over again every day of the year (24, 25).

On one day each year, the Day of Atonement (or the Day of Judgment), the sanctuary was cleansed of the accumulated sins symbolized by the sprinkled blood (26). This cleansing, like the daily service, was also done through the symbolic transfer of sins through the blood of sacrificial animals.

While the High Priest performed the cleansing ceremony, the people were to be fasting and praying and examining their own lives (27, 28). Upon completion of the cleansing process, the sin from the sanctuary was symbolically placed upon a goat called a scapegoat. The goat was then led outside of the encampment to a wilderness area where it was left to wander and die (29).

Although this is a very brief synopsis of a very complicated and beautiful service, it represented the priestly ministry of Jesus and His right through his own shed blood to represent the human race as their counsel in the court of the universe and win their redemption (30, 31).

This service also symbolized Satan as the scapegoat who ultimately must bear the responsibility of his leadership role in the experience of sin (32).

Adventists deny that the symbolism of Satan as the scapegoat carrying the guilt of the world's sins in any way detracts from the complete atonement accomplished at the cross by Jesus Christ. Jesus did indeed pay the full price for sin. Whether or not Satan would live or die, the work done by God at Calvary was sufficient to save any and all who would believe. Jesus, in the symbolic act of placing the sin which He had borne since Calvary upon the head of Satan is thereby symbolically placing the *responsibility for sin* right back where it belongs, upon its prime instigator and long-term promoter. God was in no way responsible for sin—although He paid the full penalty, the penalty of death. With the death of Satan, sin too would finally be eliminated from the universe.

In this doctrine, Adventist teaching is again unique. Most Christians who have studied the book of Hebrews in the New Testament have seen the symbolic function of the Hebrew sanctuary system. Among these, Adventists have stood relatively alone in that portion of the symbolism portrayed by the cleansing of the sanctuary on the Day of Atonement as described in the eighth chapter of the book of Daniel.

The prophecy cited identifies a time period of twenty-three hundred years after which the true sanctuary would be cleansed (33). The beginning of this prophetic period is clearly described and can be accurately pinpointed in history (34). The end point occurred in the year 1844 according to the calculations of William Miller, the leader of the movement in the early nineteenth century, a date still accepted by the rank and file of Adventism.

Miller interpreted the prophecy to indicate that the cleansing of the sanctuary referred to the cleansing of the earth by fire. It was not until after The Disappointment and further careful study of the Scriptures of both the Old and the New Testaments that it became evident that the cleansing of the sanctuary referred to the work of the risen Christ in the true sanctuary in heaven rather than to an event here on earth (Hebrews 8:1, 2). As the work of the high priest ·effectively wiped out all record of confessed sin for the

26. *Leviticus 16:16 (NEB):* "He shall make for the sanctuary the expiation required by the ritual uncleanness of the Israelites and their acts of rebellion, that is by all their sins; and he shall do the same for the Tent of the Presence, which dwells among them in the midst of all their uncleanness."

27. *Leviticus 16:29, 30, 33 (NEB):* "This shall become a rule binding on you for all time. On the tenth day of the seventh month you shall mortify yourselves; you shall do no work, whether native Israelite or alien settler, because on this day expiation shall be made on your benefit to cleanse you, and so make you clean before the Lord from all your sins ... he shall put on the sacred linen clothes and shall make expiation for the holy sanctuary, the Tent of the Presence, and the altar, on behalf of the priests and the whole assembly of the people."

28. *Leviticus 23:27 (NEB):* "... Further, the tenth day of this seventh month is the Day of Atonement. There shall be a sacred assembly; you shall mortify yourselves and present a food-offering to the Lord."

29. *Leviticus 16:10 (NEB):* "... but the goat on which the lot for the Precipice has fallen shall be made to stand alive before the Lord, for expiation to be made over it before it is driven away into the wilderness to the Precipice."

30. *Hebrews 9:26-28 (NEB):* "If that were so, he would have had to suffer many times since the world was made. But as it is, he has appeared once and for all at the climax of history to abolish sin by the sacrifice of himself. And as it is the lot of men to die once, and after death comes judgment, so Christ was offered once to bear the burden of men's sins, and will appear a second time, sin done away, to bring salvation to those who are watching for him."

31. Hebrews 10:21, 22 (NEB): "We have, moreover, a great priest set over the household of God; so let us make our approach in sincerity of heart and full assurance of faith, our guilty hearts sprinkled clean, our bodies washed with pure water."

32. Revelation 20:1-3 (NEB): "Then I saw an angel coming down from heaven with the key of the abyss and a great chain in his hands. He seized the dragon, that serpent of old, the Devil or Satan, and chained him up for a thousand years; he threw him into the abyss, shutting and sealing it over him, so that he might seduce the nations no more till the thousand years were over. After that he must be let loose for a short while."

33. Daniel 8:14 (KJV): "And he said unto me, 'Unto two thousand and three hundred days; then shall the sanctuary be cleansed."

34. Daniel 9:25 (KJV): "Know therefore and understand, that from the going forth of the commandment to restore and to build Jerusalem unto the Messiah the Prince shall be seven weeks, and threescore and two weeks: the streets shall be built again, and the wall, even in troublous times."

35. Hebrews 8:12 (NEB): "For all of them, high and low, shall know me; I will be merciful to their wicked deeds, and I will remember their sins no more."

36. I John 2:1 (NEB): "My children, in writing thus to you my purpose is that you should not commit sin. But should anyone commit a sin, we have one to plead our cause with the Father, Jesus Christ, and he is just."

37. Isaiah 43:25 (NEB): "I alone, I am He, who for his own sake wipes out your transgressions, who will remember your sins no more."

people of ancient Israel, so Christ, our High Priest, blots out our confessed sins from the books of record and thus their consequence, i.e., death (35 through 39). This is the judgment that Adventists believe is referred to in Scripture where Satan is described as standing at man's side to accuse us (Zechariah 3:1-4). It is the time that Jesus, man's advocate, takes their defense. Already, He has redeemed man by His own spilled blood and clothed him with His robe of righteousness. Those who have flourished in their life in Christ will receive the seal of God's faithful ones. But those who for one reason or another have lost their connection with the saving blood of Christ (as the seeds sown by the farmer or the branches lopped from the vine) will be found unprepared (40 through 42).

By implication, this aspect of the Judgment must occur before the Lord comes to claim His own. The record is clear that, "We must all appear before the Judgment seat of Christ, that each one may receive what is due him for the things done while in the body, whether good or bad" (II Corinthians 5:10). Adventists have referred to this as the pre-Advent judgment or investigative judgment (43, 44).

Upon completion of this aspect of judgment, the jury will give the verdict in favor of the defense. The world then will witness the return of Christ when He comes in His glory with all of the angels of heaven to gather His followers from the four corners of the earth. Those who have accepted the merits of His shed blood (i.e., the defendants) will meet the Lord in the air and be transported to heaven with Him and the vast throng of unfallen angels (45 through 48).

The wicked, destroyed by the brightness and majesty of His personal appearance in glory, will litter the earth. Then begins the wilderness experience of Satan, the scapegoat. He and his angels are confined to this earth for one thousand years as if chained in a great abyss alone to view and contemplate the terrible consequence that sin has wrought upon the world and the human race (49, 50).

During the thousand years that the redeemed are with Jesus in heaven, the Bible suggests another work of judgment, and though not specific as to the details, the Bible does suggest that it will be a judgment of angels as well as men (51, 52).

Adventists have often interpreted this as a time when the redeemed will have the opportunity to examine the record of those who are lost in order to understand why.

During this time it will be seen that God has spared no expense and withheld no effort, but has instead poured all of the resources of Heaven into His attempt to rescue the human race. All who are lost are lost because of their own choice. A patient, long-suffering, and loving God has not interfered with their free choice (53 through 55).

During this life, saints and sinners alike often wonder and struggle over the apparent inequities and injustices that plague the human race. But on that great day, all will become plain to the judging saints and it will be determined that God has acted correctly (56).

At the end of the thousand years, the wicked and rebellious of all generations will be raised to life again upon the earth in time to see the Holy City with Jesus and the redeemed returning from heaven. Arising with the same spirit with which they died, and marshalled by the same power of Satan that controlled them previously, they will think that their greater numbers can overpower and capture the Holy City (57 through 59).

At that point Jesus (as King of Kings and Lord of Lords) will stand in all of His glory before all of His creation, saint and sinner alike, and as He privately revealed the secrets of the hearts of the Jews who brought to Him the woman caught in adultery (John 8:1-11), so He will reveal the hearts and secret sins, the motives and the acts to each and every individual who is lost.

At that time, each sinner will understand the rebellion of his own heart and see the answers to the questions that he refused to acknowledge in his former life. And when confronted with the evidence, each lost person will bow before the King of the Universe and acknowledge His rightful power (60, 61).

God's love requires that every intelligent being fully understand the issues and acknowledge in his own heart his own incompatability with the environment of heaven. There will be none there who are incapable of harmonizing with Heaven's principles. Adventists understand this to be the reason for the resurrection of the wicked.

The Bible describes the next event as the death of Satan and all of his followers, both angelic and

38. Revelation 3:5 (NEB): "He who is victorious shall thus be robed all in white; his name I will never strike off the roll of the living, for in the presence of my Father and his angels I will acknowledge him as mine."

39. II Corinthians 1:22 (NEB): ". . . it is God also who has set his seal upon us, and as a pledge of what is to come has given the Spirit to dwell in our hearts."

40. Revelation 7:2,3 (NEB): "Then I saw another angel rising out of the east, carrying the seal of the Living God; and he called aloud to the four angels who had been given the power to ravage land and sea. Do no damage to sea or land or trees until we have set the seal of God upon the forehead of his servants."

41. John 15:6 (NEB): "He who does not dwell in me is thrown away like a withered branch. The withered branches are heaped together, thrown on the fire, and burnt."

42. Leviticus 23:29 (NEB): "Therefore, every person who does not mortify himself on that day shall be cut off from his father's kin."

43. I Thessalonians 4:16 (NEB): ". . . because at the word of command, at the sound of the archangel's voice and God's trumpet-call, the Lord himself will descend from heaven."

44. I Peter 4:17 (NEB): "The time has come for the judgment to begin; it is beginning with God's own household. And if it is starting with you, how will it end for those who refuse to obey the gospel of God?"

45. Luke 21:27 (NEB): "And then they will see the Son of Man coming on a cloud with great power and glory."

46. Matthew 16:27 (NEB): "For the Son of Man is to come in the glory of his Father with his angels, and then he will give

**47. Matthew 25:32, 33
(NEB):** "When the Son of
Man comes in his glory
and all the angels with
him, he will sit in state on
his throne, with all the
nations gathered before
him. He will separate men
into two groups, as a shepherd separates the sheep
from the goats, and he
will place the sheep on
his right hand and the
goats on his left."

48. Mark 8:38 (NEB):
"What can he give to buy
that self back? If anyone
is ashamed of me and
mine in this wicked and
godless age, the Son of
Man will be ashamed of
him, when he comes in
the glory of his Father
and of the holy angels."

**49. Leviticus 16:21, 22
(NEB):** "He shall lay both
his hands on its head and
confess over it all the iniquities of the Israelites and
all their acts of rebellion,
that is all their sins; he
shall lay them on the head
of the goat and send it
away into the wilderness
in charge of a man who is
waiting ready. The goat
shall carry all their iniquities upon itself into
some barren waste and
the man shall let it go,
there in the wilderness."

**50. Revelation 20:2, 3
(NEB):** "He seized the dragon, that serpent of old,
the Devil or Satan, and
chained him up for a thousand years; he threw him
into the abyss, shutting
and sealing it over him,
so that he might seduce
the nations no more till
the thousand years were
over. After that he must
be let loose for a short
while."

**51. I Corinthians 6:2, 3
(NIV):** "Do you not know
that the saints will judge
the world? And if you are
to judge the world, are
you not competent to
judge trivial cases? Do
you not know that we will
judge angels? How much
more the things of this
life!"

52. Revelation 20:4 (NIV):
"I saw thrones on which
were seated those who
had been given authority
to judge. And I saw the

human, by the fires that cleanse the earth and prepare
it for recreation to its former state to become the home
of the redeemed for all ages to come (62 through 65).

It is true that the Bible speaks of fires that cannot be
quenched. But a careful study of those scriptures
reveals very clearly that they describe a fire that consumes and destroys and whose results are eternal.
They do not describe a fire that burns forever. Sin and
sinners and all evidence of the wickedness of this
earth will be destroyed. About this the Bible is clear.
(66) (Fudge, 1982).

But the Bible presents no basis in fact to defend the
teaching that God allows or enjoys torturing those
whom He has given His life to rescue. Some might
even question whether a loving God could destroy any
of His creation—even those given over to sin. The
evidence suggests that under the right circumstances,
even death may be a merciful act of a loving God (67).

Six thousand years of sin have demonstrated that to
live in an environment of sin may be worse in many
ways than death itself. Its eternal continuation has no
meaning and purpose. Since the wicked will have
rejected all efforts at reconciliation, there will be no
other choices available (68, 69).

Many Adventists expect that day to be a very emo-
tionally packed experience as the redeemed witness
the final destruction of many of those whom they have
loved while on earth. They expect that God and the
angels of heaven will also be shedding tears of sadness. But mixed with these tears will be joy and rejoicing, for all will realize that at last the universe is secure
and sin and evil will never again show their ugly faces
(70).

Sorrow, pain, and death will be banished forever
(71).

The Bible is full of instances where judgment has
been executed in the name of God. Classic examples
are the worldwide flood at the time of Noah, the destruction of Sodom and Gomorrah at the time of Abraham, the ten plagues and drowning of Pharoah and
his army at the time of the Exodus, and the conquest of
the Israelites and their subsequent captivity by the
Babylonians.

In the Book of Job the curtains are drawn aside and
reveal that all acts that appear to be acts of God are in
reality the consequences of the struggle between good
and evil that are occurring behind the scenes (72, 73).

God's ultimate purpose of restoring the race must be accomplished at any cost. Satan is not easily discouraged in his attempt to thwart God's plan.

While at times—in the name of freedom—God has had to withhold His life-sustaining hand and allow the consequences of evil to accomplish their destructive purposes, Satan has himself created catastrophe and destruction and placed the blame upon God.

Ultimately, since God is the ruler of the universe, He must bear the responsibility for a given act whether it be the withholding of His own power of support or whether by allowing Satan to exercise his power. From a human perspective it is difficult to distinguish the two. It is sometimes difficult to understand the record of history as being administered by a loving God. But when looked at from the view that God is the sustainer of this world and that it is by His power that it continues to function day by day, then one realizes that the mere withholding of His power allows the natural course of evil to occur. It is this that many Adventists interpret as the judgment and wrath of God.

They suggest that one day when there is opportunity to look back over the course of history and review it from the perspective of Heaven and the plan of God, the redeemed will finally be able to understand how every event that has transpired in human history has occurred in the context of love and God's desire for the restoration of our race (74).

This picture of Judgment in the context of the controversy between good and evil, between God and Satan, is a vital foundation stone of Adventist teaching and belief. Many other Christians acknowledge this Biblical concept in principal, yet fail to see the beauty of the details of the plan of God as Adventists teach. Adventists believe that this doctrine is the secret to a rational understanding of many otherwise difficult and paradoxical Biblical statements and say it provides them with a picture of true love that nothing else can do.

To the Adventist mind, the events of Judgment as herein outlined are very easily defensible by a careful study of the Holy Scriptures. To them, the Scriptures paint a beautiful picture of God's long-suffering, His mercy, and His justice, and provide answers to many of the questions asked by the human race for six thousand years about sadness and sorrow and death.

souls of those who had been beheaded because of their testimony for Jesus and because of the work of God. They had not worshipped the beast or his image and had not received his mark on their foreheads or their hands. They came to life and reigned with Christ a thousand years."

53. II Peter 3:9 (NEB): "It is not that the Lord is slow in fulfilling his promise, as some suppose, but that he is very patient with you, because it is not his will for any to be lost, but for all to come to repentance."

54. John 3:19 (NEB): "Here lies the test: the light has come into the world, but men preferred darkness to light because their deeds were evil."

55. Deuteronomy 30:19 (NEB): "I summon heaven and earth to witness against you this day: I offer you the choice of life or death, blessing or curse."

56. Revelation 15:3, 4 (NEB): "They were singing the song of Moses, the servant of God, and the song of the lamb, as they chanted: 'Great and marvellous are thy deeds, O Lord God, sovereign over all; just and true are thy ways, thou king of the ages. Who shall not revere thee, Lord, and do homage to thy name? For thou alone art holy. All nations shall come and worship in thy presence, for thy just dealings stand revealed.'"

57. Revelation 20:5 (NEB): "... though the rest of the dead did not come to life until the thousand years were over."

58. John 5:29 (NEB): "... those who have done right will rise to life; those who have done wrong will rise to hear their doom."

59. Revelation 20:9 (NEB): "So they marched over the breadth of the land and laid siege to the camp of God's people and the city that he loves."

31

60. Romans 14:11 (NEB): "For Scripture says, 'As I live, says the Lord, to me every knee shall bow and every tongue acknowledge God.'"

61. Isaiah 45:23 (NEB): "By my life I have sworn, I have given a promise of victory, a promise that will not be broken, that to me every knee shall bend and by me every tongue shall swear."

62. Revelation 20:9,10 (NEB): "But fire came down them from heaven and consumed them; and the Devil, their seducer, was flung into the lake of fire and sulphur, where the beast and the false prophet had been flung, there to be tomented day and night forever."

63. Revelation 20:14, 15 (NEB): "Then Death and Hades were flung into the lake of fire. This lake of fire is the second death; and into it were flung any whose names were not to be found in the roll of the living."

64. II Peter 3:13 (NEB): "But we have his promise, and look forward to new heavens and a new earth, the home of justice."

65. Revelation 21:1 (NEB): "Then I saw a new heaven and a new earth, for the first heaven and the first earth had vanished, and there was no longer any sea."

66. II Peter 3:10, 12 (NEB): "But the day of the Lord will come; it will come, unexpected as a thief. On that day the heavens will disappear with a great rushing sound, the elements will disintegrate in flames, and the earth with all that is in it will be laid bare . . . Look eagerly for the coming of the Day of God and work to hasten it on; that day will set the heavens ablaze until they fall apart, and will melt the elements in flames."

67. Isaiah 28:21 (NEB): "But the Lord shall arise as he rose on Mount Perazim and storm with rage as he did in the Vale of Gibeon to do what he must do—how strange a deed! to perform his work—how outlandish a work!"

68. Psalms 81:12 (NEB): ". . . so I sent them off, stubborn as they were, to follow their own devices."

69. Romans 1:21, 28 (NEB): "There is therefore no possible defense for their conduct; knowing God, they have refused to honour him as God, or to render him thanks. Hence all their thinking has ended in futility, and their misguided minds are plunged in darkness . . . Thus, because they have not seen fit to acknowledge God, he has given them up to their own depraved reason. This leads them to break all rules of conduct."

70. Ezekiel 33:11 (NEB): "So tell them: As I live, says the Lord God, I have no desire for the death of the wicked. I would rather that a wicked man should mend his ways and live. Give up your evil ways, give them up; O Israelites, why should you die?"

71. Revelation 21:4 (NEB): "He will wipe every tear from their eyes; there shall be an end to death, and to mourning and crying and pain; for the old order has passed away!"

72. Job 1:9-12 (NEB): "Satan answered the Lord, 'Has not Job good reason to be God-fearing? Have you not hedged him round on every side with your protection, him and his family and all his possessions? Whatever he does you have blessed, and his herds have increased beyond measure. But stretch out your hand and touch all that he has, and then he will curse you to your face.' Then the Lord said to Satan, 'So be it. All that he has is in your hands; only Job himself you must not touch.' And Satan left the Lord's presence."

73. Job 2:7 (NEB): "And Satan left the Lord's presence, and he smote Job with running sores from head to foot . . ."

74. Romans 8:28 (NEB): ". . . and in everything, as we know, he cooperates for good with those who love God and are called according to his purpose."

Adventists find it difficult to understand how they can be criticized and condemned for believing and teaching a doctrine with such meaning, especially when Scripture seems to support it so well. Still, Adventists have departed from traditional Christian thought in certain aspects of this doctrine. Because of these departures, some believe that the cult designation is necessary. Does the Biblical evidence support such incrimination?

REFERENCE

Fudge, Edward W. The Fire that Consumes. *Houston, TX: Providential Press, 1982.*

32

Chapter V

Legalism:
Keepers of the Law

One of the teachings that has been most responsible for including Adventists among those groups labeled cults is the teaching of the necessity for obedience to God's laws. From earliest times, this obedience has been viewed by much of the Christian world as legalism. Because Adventists teach that the Ten Commandments are as much the law of God now as they were when given to Israel many years ago, it is reasoned that Adventists are denying the work of Christ on the cross. Other ideas regarding diet, entertainment, adornment, and similar lifestyle practices sometimes make it appear that Adventists are bound by an even tighter set of laws and rules than were the ancient Jews. This concern for obedience to the commandments seems to confirm the indictment. But how can this be if they believe in the atoning sacrifice of Jesus? That is the question! Most Christians would agree that if Adventists deny the work of Christ in their actions, if not in their words, they ought not be considered Christian, and do thereby deserve the designation of a "cult."

What are the facts?

According to Webster's Unabridged Dictionary, legalism refers to "the doctrine of salvation by good works." (Webster, 1979.) In other words, a legalist attempts to keep the law and to do good things in order to be saved and go to heaven when he dies.

New Testament Scripture teaches quite clearly that this is NOT the way to get to heaven "... no man is ever justified by doing what the law demands, but only through faith in Christ," (Galatians 2:16, NEB); for "if righteousness comes by law, then Christ died for nothing" (Galatians 2:21, NEB).

Adventists claim that they believe in the atoning work of Christ on the cross. They believe that they trust in it, but do they? Or are they self-deceived? Do they indeed practice legalism and thereby make "for nothing" the death of Christ as so many would allege?

To unravel this mystery, it will be essential to explore the Scriptural basis for Adventist beliefs as they relate to the issue at hand. This study will begin with an examination of the concept of law as viewed by the Adventist mind.

What is law?

The term law is used in many different ways. For purposes here, the term describes the principles that govern God's creation. These may be seen as: 1) those principles of cause and effect that God designed and by which His Creation functions; 2) the rules and statutes that describe, instruct, commemorate, and, in other ways, apply the principles and allow people to live comfortably within these cause and effect principles. The first set of laws are permanent and unchangeable. They include the laws that govern such things as physics, mathematics, etc. For example, at a given atmospheric pressure, water always boils at 100 degrees Celsius. But these laws are broader than physical conditions and govern more than inanimate things. These laws also govern the animate and intelligent creations of God.

God did not create intelligent creatures to live and operate apart from the laws that would assure their continued existance. Rather, He created them to function according to prescribed laws which govern social and spiritual relations with one another, and with Him, as well as laws governing the physical functions. All of these are cause and effect laws. A given action causes a predictable result. When living in accordance with these laws, a person is often not even aware of their existence. But if he ignores and disregards them, he gets hurt. For example, stepping off the edge of a cliff subjects one to the effects of gravity punishment for ignoring her effects. Just as by disregarding laws, an injury may occur, so by obedience, benefit will be realized. It is the same with social and spiritual laws as with physical laws.

Furthermore, it is not the fact that one believes and obeys a given doctrine or law that causes God to look with favor upon someone or reward one for goodness. Instead, laws are the vehicles or channels through which blessing (or salvation) may come. For example, what happens if one chooses to disregard the commandment regarding adultery (1). Jesus said that to even look at a woman to lust after her was as good as committing the act. But God does not slam the pearly gates for either the looking or the doing. Rather, if someone loses the precious inheritance, it will be because of what effect disregard for this law will have

1. *Matthew 5:28 (NEB):* *"But what I tell you is this: if a man looks on a woman with a lustful eye, he has already committed adultery with her in his heart."*

34

upon both the individual who sins and upon society around him. The broken home resulting from the adultrous act may destroy his children. It may forever discourage his spouse. And it may contribute to the final destruction of the family unit as one of the vital foundation stones of society. And, yes, all of these may irreversibly disrupt the ability of the disobedient one to respond to God's saving grace while attempting to deal with and justify his actions. So it is with all of God's commands. Obedience yields life. Disobedience yields death by natural consequence.

When Moses led the people of Israel out of Egypt on the way to the Promised Land, God gave them a code of laws on how to function. This code was composed of laws from both categories: cause and effect laws, and rules and statutes. Adventists believe that the great principles governing the expression of love—The Ten Commandments—are of the first category. They are cause and effect laws, and they are eternal and unchanging. Before sin entered the world, intelligent creation lived in compliance with them by nature, being totally unconscious of their existence.

The other laws of Moses, the rules and statutes, were also given by God, but were of a different nature. They belonged to several categories. Some detailed the daily application of the Great Commandments. They described how the Commandments were to be applied in particular situations. Others governed the health of the community and the individual. Some others were commemorative in nature and reminded the Jews of their deliverance from Egyptian bondage. Still others pointed toward their ultimate deliverance when God Himself would die as their ransomed sacrifice and restore them again to God's image as before the Fall. These latter laws were flexible and situational and, in many instances, served a timely purpose (2).

Upon initial reading of the Bible, there appear to be inconsistencies regarding the law in the New Testament. Jesus is quoted as saying that, "I have not come to destroy the law but to fulfill it" (3). Paul in his letter to the church at Colossia talks about setting the law aside and nailing it to the cross (4). Based on careful attention to the Scriptural intent as determined by context and Biblical theme, and with consideration to the nature of law, these two texts are not in any way contradictory, but are rather complimentary. Both types of laws found fulfillment and both were in one

2. *Hebrews 10:1 (NEB):* "*For the law contains but a shadow, and no true image, of the good things to come . . .*"

3. *Matthew 5:17, 18 (NIV):* "*Do not think that I have come to abolish the Law or the Prophets; I have not come to abolish them but to fulfill them. I tell you the truth, until heaven and earth disappear, not the smallest letter, not the least stroke of a pen, will by any means disappear from the Law until everything is accomplished.*"

4. *Colossians 2:14 (NEB):* "*He has cancelled the bond which pledged us to the decrees of the law. It stood against us, but he has set it aside, nailing it to the cross.*"

5. *Hebrews 9:9, 10 (NEB):* "All this is symbolic, pointing to the present time. The offerings and sacrifices there prescribed cannot give the worshipper inward perfection. It is only a matter of food and drink and various rights of cleansing—outward ordinances in force until the time of reformation."

6. *I Peter 2:21 (NIV):* "To this you were called, because Christ suffered for you, leaving you an example, that you should follow in His steps."

7. *Hebrews 8:1-6 (NEB):* "Now this is my main point: just such a high priest we have, and he has taken his seat at the right hand of the throne of Majesty in the heavens, a ministrant in the real sanctuary, the tent pitched by the Lord and not by man. Every high priest is appointed to offer gifts and sacrifices; hence, this one too must have something to offer. Now if he had been on earth, he would not even have been a priest, since there are already priests who offer the gifts which the Law prescribes, though they minister in a sanctuary which is only a copy and shadow of the heavenly. This is implied when Moses, about to erect the tent, is instructed by God: 'See to it that you make everything according to the pattern shown you on the mountain.' But, in fact, the ministry which has fallen to Jesus is as far superior to theirs as are the covenant he mediates and the promises upon which it is legally secured."

8. *Hebrews 10:9, 10 (NEB):* "He thus annuls the former to establish the latter. And it is by the will of God that we have been consecrated, through the offering of the body of Jesus Christ, once and for all."

9. *John 14:15, 21 (NEB):* "If you love me, you will obey my commands . . . The man who has received my commands and obeys them—he it is who loves me; and he who loves me will be loved by my Father; and I will love him and disclose myself to him."

sense set aside in Jesus' death on the cross.

Not only did those ceremonial laws pointing to the Lamb of God find fulfillment in Jesus' death as type met antitype, but the Great Commandments themselves found fulfillment as Jesus showed us how to live by love (5, 6), and thereby gave us an example to emulate. In the sense that Jesus taught obedience through the power of love and gave us the incentive to do so, the law was nailed to the cross (Titus 2:12). No longer did people have an excuse to attempt to obey the law to gain God's favor.

From now on, obedience would be the response of love, not selfish desire for reward.

In another sense, the rules and statutes were also nailed to the cross. Those ceremonial laws pointing toward the work of Jesus' atonement were no longer applicable. These were in effect done away with, nailed to the tree. Other rules and regulations especially pertinent to their time and needs were outdated and were no longer needed (7, 8). But, in no sense were the principles contained in the Ten Commandments done away with, for God is love, and these laws are the expression of love in action (Mark 12:28-34) (Thompson, 1988, 19-24).

Traditional Seventh-day Adventist doctrine teaches that it is possible to be obedient to the Commandments in both word and spirit—to live a righteous life with victory over sin (9 through 11). In fact, Adventists believe and teach that all who live at the end of time (the remnant) and who proclaim the "Third Angel's message" (sometimes referred to as the "Elijah Message" and the message of "Righteousness by Faith"— more about these terms later) will be obedient. Those who are sealed with the seal of God when the sealing angel is sent from heaven to identify God's own, are described as, "those who keep the commandments of God and have the faith of Jesus" (Revelation 14:12).

From this it is clear that righteousness is a condition that Adventists believe is attainable and that they believe is related to obedience to the commandments of God. However, they are very careful to point out that the righteousness that they profess is a righteousness made possible only through faith in Christ and the merits of His sacrifice on the cross and His continued ministry as High Priest in the heavenly sanctuary. According to Adventists, righteousness cannot be attained by doing the works of the law, even though

36

the law is involved.

What does it mean to live a righteous life by faith, to be victorious over sin? Just this! To be righteous (good) by faith is essentially equivalent to being righteous by believing. Believing in what? Believing in the Gospel! The Gospel states that, "God so loved the world that He gave His only begotten son that whosoever believeth in Him shall not perish, but have everlasting life" (John 3:16).

But what is there about believing the Gospel that makes one righteous? Is it an act of magic that God performs when a person "accepts" Jesus or receives the "New Birth"? Or does it occur when a man dies and goes to heaven on resurrection morning (12)? No! It is a miraculous change that occurs in one's heart (mind) when one comprehends the beauty of the great cost paid by God for his ransom (13). In the truest sense, it is really birth to a new way of life (14 through 22). Not only does the Gospel teach that God loves enough to forgive man's foolishness and outright evil, but it also declares that God is interested enough to offer everything heaven has to give in order to rescue him from certain destruction caused by sin and to restore His creation again to His image (23 through 28).

If God is this kind of god, how can anyone refuse such love and goodness? If one truly believes this Gospel, is it possible to stand idly by while Satan and the powers of evil, either unseen or seen, attack and seek to destroy the principles and the people for whom Jesus died?

Can a person continue to support those distortions of truth that bring dishonor to the name of God? Can he share those attitudes, actions, and lifestyle practices that are at war against God?

The answer is a resounding, "NO!" if one truly believes. In other words, believing results in obedience to those principles that man's lover espouses, i.e., patience, long-suffering, goodness, and justice—the characteristics of love (Exodus 34:6,7; John 3:16). True belief leads to an abhorrence for evil whenever and where ever that evil is revealed for what it is.

This is what it means to be righteous by faith. This is the meaning of the expression, "Christ in you, the hope of glory" (Colossians 1:27). Jesus forgives transgressions; He draws man with His love; He empowers man with His Spirit to change human natures in order to bring actions into conformity with beliefs. This

10. *I John 2:3-6 (NEB):* *"Here is the test by which we can make sure that we know him: do we keep his commands? The man who says, 'I know him, while he disobeys his commands, is a liar and a stranger to the truth; but in the man who is obedient to his word, the divine love has indeed come to its perfection. Here is the test by which we can make sure that we are in him: whoever claims to be dwelling in him, binds himself to live as Christ himself lived."*

11. *I John 3:24 (NEB):* *"When we keep his commands, we dwell in him and he dwells in us. And this is how we can make sure that he dwells within us: we know it from the Spirit he has given us."*

12. *Matthew 7:21 (NEB):* *"Not everyone who calls me, 'Lord, Lord,' will enter the kingdom of Heaven, but only those who do the will of my heavenly Father."*

13. *II Corinthians 5:14, 15, 17 (NEB):* *"For the love of Christ leaves us no choice, when once we have reached the conclusion that one man died for all and therefore all mankind has died. His purpose in dying for all was that man, while still in life, should cease to live for themselves, and should live for him who for their sake died and was raised to life . . . When anyone is united to Christ, there is a new world; the old order has gone, and a new order has already begun."*

14. *II Corinthians 4:6 (NEB):* *"For the same God who said, 'Out of darkness, let light shine,' has caused his light to shine within us, to give the light of revelation—the revelation of the glory of God in the face of Jesus Christ."*

15. *Galatians 2:20 (NEB):* *"I have been crucified with Christ: the life I now live is not my life, but the life which Christ lives in me; and my present bodily life is lived by faith in the Son of God, who loved me and gave himself up for me."*

16. Ephesians 3:17-19
(NEB): ". . . that through
faith Christ may dwell in
your hearts in love. With
deep roots and firm foun-
dations, may you be
strong to grasp, with all
God's people, what is the
breadth and length and
height and depth of the
love of Christ, and to
know it, though it is be-
yond knowledge. So may
you attain to fullness of
being, the fullness of God
himself."

17. John 15:3 (NEB):
"You have already been
cleansed by the word that
I spoke to you. Dwell in
me, as I in you."

18. II Peter 1:3, 4 (NEB):
"His divine power has be-
stowed on us everything
that makes for life and
true religion, enabling us
to know the One who
called us by his own
splendour and might.
Through this might and
splendour he has given us
his promises, great be-
yond all price, and
through them you may
escape the corruption
with which lust has in-
fected the world, and
come to share in the very
being of God."

19. John 3:5 (NEB):
"Jesus answered, 'In
truth I tell you, no one
can enter the kingdom of
God without being born
from water and spirit.'"

20. John 15:4, 10 (NEB):
"Dwell in me, as I in you.
No branch can bear fruit
by itself, but only if it
remains united with the
vine; no more can you
bear fruit, unless you remain united with me . .
Dwell in my love. If you
heed my commands, you
will dwell in my love, as I
have heeded my Father's
commands and dwell in
his love."

21. Romans 12:2 (NEB):
"Adapt yourselves no
longer to the pattern of
this present world, but
let your minds be remade
and your whole nature
thus transformed. Then
you will be able to dis-
cern the will of God, and
to know what is good,
acceptable, and perfect."

alignment of beliefs and lives is God's solution to the sin problem. People thus transformed will be "safe to save."

The process is a struggle for every sinner (29). Human nature is very accustomed to evil. Man has inherited many evil propensities. These are ingrained into the genetic code. In addition, from earliest child-hood, he has an environment where evil predominates and takes on many of the habits and characteristics of that environment just by being a part of it. It is a law of the mind that by beholding we become changed. More than that, sin is exciting. It is pleasant and enjoyable. It caters to our senses and to our emotions. Satan has so cunningly wrapped his packages that evil has the appearance of good—so good that it is difficult to resist—even after the whole evil plot of Satan to cap-ture by his enticements is revealed.

Though the struggle is real and sometimes almost overwhelming, there is assurance of victory. Advent-ists believe that being righteous by faith as thus des-cribed is not legalism. It is not obeying the law for desire of reward. It is, rather, merely the expression of the love that fills the whole being after the Gospel accomplishes its work on a person. It is the "Law written upon the heart" (Hebrews 10:16). Even rules and statutes have value when obeyed in love. There are many rules that Seventh-day Adventists have that have been interpreted as legalistic. For example, Seventh-day Adventists accept Paul's teaching writ-ten to the Corinthians that the body is the temple of the living God (30, 31). As such, it is to be embellished with Christian virtues and protected from destructive practices. Adventists understand that many of the health laws spoken by God through Moses are as valid today as when first given (32, 33) (McMillen). They believe, for example, that the ideal diet consists of the menu prescribed by the Creator in the beginning, and that meat and animal products are not an essential component of health under most circumstances (34). Instead, they generally represent indulgence to appe-tite (Galations 5:24, I John 2:16).

Such indulgence often leads to illness and prema-ture death. More importantly, it interferes with spirit-ual perception and response. In keeping with the love for God and the desire to maintain as far as possible a suitable temple for His indwelling, health practices are an important component of Adventist philosophy.

Ellen White states in *Counsels on Diet and Foods:* "You need clear, energetic minds in order to appreciate the exalted character of truth, to value the atonement, and to place the right estimate upon eternal things. If you persue a wrong course, and indulge in wrong habits of eating, and thereby weaken the intellectual powers, you will not place that high estimate upon salvation and eternal life which will inspire you to conform your life to the life of Christ." (White, 1946, 47.)

As in all aspects of Christian growth, these health laws may also sometimes be obeyed legalistically. Other teachings dealing with Christian behavior in dress, ornamentation, entertainment, business practices, and a whole host of similar activities, may likewise be obeyed from either a legalistic perspective or a love motive (35 through 38). Which reason governs a believer's choice depends upon his or her individual level of growth and relationship with his Lord. One may look at such a growing Christian and judge him as being legalistically conservative or possibly even embarrassingly liberal without really understanding the motive of the heart. Jesus admonished that we, "Judge not" (39).

Adventists believe that they can lead a life according to the motive of love. They believe that by the power of Jesus they can live the kind of life He lived when He was a man among men. As He overcame evil by total dependence upon His Father, so they can overcome. Adventists firmly believe that the same kind of self-sacrificing love that dominates the heart of God can come to dominate and control the life of human beings if they will commit their lives to Him without reservation (40, 41).

But what if one wants to believe but is not willing to give himself up completely to the indwelling of love? What if one prefers instead a measure of self-expression and the relatively comfortable life found on the easier path (Matthew 7:13)? What if one is not ready to yield up the pleasures of sin? What if one is unwilling (even with God's assurance of victory) to struggle against the evils inherent in our human nature and to gain the victory?

In this case, one of two alternatives frequently occurs. First, the individual can distort the truth about the process of the work of grace and tell himself that God has done it all through Christ without any human involvement. This suggests God will save man no

22. Matthew 7:13, 14 (NEB): "Enter by the narrow gate. The gate is wide that leads to perdition, there is plenty of room on the road, and many go that way; but the gate that leads to life is small and the road is narrow, and those who find it are few."

23. John 13:1 (NEB): "It was before the Passover festival. Jesus knew that his hour had come and he must leave this world and go to the Father. He had always loved his own who were in the world, and now he was to show the full extent of his love."

24. Jude 24, 25 (NEB): "Now to the One who can keep you from falling and set you in the presence of his glory, jubilant and above reproach, to the only God our Saviour, be glory and majesty, might and authority, through Jesus Christ our Lord, before all time, now, and for evermore. Amen."

25. John 14:16, 17 (NEB): "And I will ask the Father, and he will give you another to be your Advocate, who will be with you forever—the Spirit of truth.' The world cannot receive him, because the world neither sees nor knows him; but you know him, because he dwells with you and is in you."

26. Hebrews 10:16 (NEB): "This is the covenant which I will make with them after those days, says the Lord: I will set my laws in their hearts and write them on their understanding."

27. I Corinthians 10:13 (NEB): "So far you have faced no trial beyond what man can bear. God keeps faith, and he will not allow you to be tested above your powers, but when the test comes he will at the same time provide a way out, by enabling you to sustain it."

28. Phillipians 4:13 (NEB): "I have strength for anything through him who gives me power."

29. I Corinthians 9:27 (NEB): "I bruise my own body and make it know its master, for fear that after preaching to others I should find myself rejected."

30. I Corinthians 3:16 (NEB): "Surely you know that you are God's temple, where the spirit of God dwells."

31. I Corinthians 6:19, 20 (NEB): "Do you not know that your body is a shrine of the indwelling Holy Spirit, and the Spirit is God's gift to you? You do not belong to yourselves; you were bought at a price. Then honour God in your body."

32. Deuteronomy 6:24 (NEB): "The Lord commanded us to observe all these statutes and to fear the Lord our God; it will be for us to observe all these statutes and to fear the Lord our God; it will be for our own good at all times, and he will continue to preserve our lives."

33. Deuteronomy 7:12, 15 (NEB): "If you listen to these laws and are careful to observe them then the Lord your God will observe the sworn covenant he made with your forefathers and will keep faith with you. The Lord will take away all sickness from you; He will not bring upon you any of the foul diseases of Egypt which know so well . . "

34. Genesis 1:29 (NEB): "God also said, 'I give you all plants that bear seed everywhere on earth, and every tree bearing fruit which yields seed: they shall be yours for food."

35. I Peter 3:3, 4 (NEB): "Your beauty should reside, not in outward adornment-the braiding of the hair, or jewellery, or dress—but in the inmost centre of your being, with its imperishable ornament, a gentle, quiet spirit, which is of high value in the sight of God."

36. I Timothy 2:9 (NEB): "Women again must dress in becoming manner, modestly and soberly."

matter what he does so long as he "believes." Or, on the other hand, man can attempt to do the works of the law (i.e., attempt to obey the law and make himself righteous—a deception just as real and just as dangerous as the first choice. No man can obey the law or do the works of the spirit of the law with just his own power and strength.) It is upon this point that many people get trapped, not only Adventists. Adventists may be at increased risk of getting caught doing things to gain salvation because of their concepts and their high ideals of righteousness by faith, but other Christians and non-Christians as well can also succumb to this incorrect belief. It is a characteristic of human nature to believe in one's self-sufficiency. But this risk does not defeat God's purpose.

All of the New Testament writers recognized that Christian experience is a struggle against evil (Romans 7:20). They realized that oneness with Christ (growth) is a gradual process that lasts throughout one's lifetime. This process is sometimes referred to as sanctification.

New Christians full of desire to serve their Lord, but lacking some of the experience of walking with Christ, may indeed sometimes act from motives other than pure agape love. Again, this is human nature showing through, but it does not indicate a fallacy in the process. Instead, it is a fact that obedience to defined law must often precede the ultimate Christian response in which love is the sole motivating source of obedience.

Certainly children must be taught the essentials of Christian behavior before they are sufficiently mature to experience unreserved Christian love. Even though the simple trusting faith of a child is an essential characteristic of all who would enter into the kingdom of God, children may not always obey because of love. At what point in the life obedience changes from a legal requirement to an act of love depends upon each individual and his willingness to follow the Master.

Some may make this transition early in life. Others may never make it and may live out their lives blindly obedient to a prescribed set of laws.

In short, Adventists believe that salvation is entirely the work of Christ and the cross and the things it has wrought. Those passages in Scripture that teach that believing in Jesus is the sole necessity for salvation are viewed by Adventists to be correct. But they are correct only insofar as that belief is real, to the extent

40

that it consumes the whole life and renders it totally into the control of the One in whom they profess to believe. Anything less than this is self-deception. (No one who believes that his country is at risk of invasion by another will stand idly by without defending it with his life if need be. Belief always causes action!)

Adventists do not believe or teach that they are the only ones who believe and live godly lives. Many throughout Christendom in all of its various factions love God supremely and serve Him faithfully. Adventists also believe that there are among non-Christians of all faiths those who are faithful to God and to the principles of love that they have been able to discern in the beauties of His created works (Romans 1:20). Many of these people are living righteous lives to the best of their available knowledge. They will not be found wanting in the final judgment (Romans 2:14, 15).

But having acknowledged this verity, Adventists believe that they have an end-time message that needs to be heard by the world, including those who already love their Lord. For, as will be examined later, the days which will shortly come to pass are believed to require a "faith that works" under the most trying of circumstances.

One last question needs to be addressed. How do Adventists understand the process whereby one becomes righteous by faith in Christ? Jesus said, "Ye must be born again" (John 3:7). Adventists believe that this is the starting place. When a person sees a picture of God in all of His beauty as most gloriously portrayed on the cross, he is drawn toward that beauty. The Holy Spirit then continues His work of conviction of sin, opening the mind to wisdom and the understanding of the Scriptures, and creates within one a longing to be with Christ (if it is not resisted). Adventists believe each person has to make a decision to accept His gift and follow Jesus. It must be a complete decision, unreserved. That decision, when real, will lead one to search the Scriptures in an earnest quest for truth. It will cause him to desire the presence of Jesus in his life every new day and will direct him so far as possible to avoid the things of the world. And when hard-pressed by Satan and the agents of evil with trial and temptation, he will battle diligently and faithfully—often spending long hours upon his knees in prayer (Ephesians 6:10-18). Then, when confronted with the needs of the world, and the hurting and pain of his fellow human beings, the blessings that have filled his life will flow out unchecked in service and in self-sacrificing love. This is righteousness by faith, and this

37. II Corinthians 9:7,8 (NEB): "Each person should give as he has decided for himself; there should be no reluctance, no sense of compulsion; God loves a cheerful giver. And it is in God's power to provide you richly with every good gift; thus you will have ample means in yourselves to meet each and every situation, with enough to spare for every good cause."

38. II Corinthians 6:14-16 (NEB): "Do not unite yourselves with unbelievers; they are not fit mates for you. What has righteousness to do with wickedness? Can light consort with darkness? Can Christ agree with Belial, or a believer join hand with an unbeliever? Can there be a compact between the temple of God and the idols of the heathen? And the temple of the living God is what we are. God's own words are: 'I will live and move about among them; I will be their God, and they shall be my people.'"

39. Matthew 7:1, 2 (NEB): "Pass no judgement, and you will not be judged. For as you judge others, so you will yourselves be judged, and whatever measure you deal out to others will be dealt back to you."

40. Mark 8:34-38 (NEB): "Then he called the people to him, as well as his disciples, and said to them, 'Anyone who wishes to be a follower of mine must leave self behind; he must take up his cross, and come with me. Whoever cares for his own safety is lost; but if a man will let himself be lost for my sake and for the Gospel, that man is safe. What does a man gain by winning the whole world at the cost of his true self? What can he give to buy that self back? If anyone is ashamed of me and mine in this wicked and godless age, the Son of Man will be ashamed of him, when he comes in the glory of his Father and of the holy angels.'"

41. Matthew 7:21 (NEB): "Not everyone who calls me 'Lord, Lord' will enter the kingdom of Heaven, but only those who do the will of my heavenly Father.'"

is the process by which it occurs. It is a work of Christ from beginning to end. But Christ's work cannot be complete until one decides to accept his freely offered gift.

The process of choosing may be instantaneous; or it may build slowly to a final choice. The course of change is often a gradual progression as the Spirit of God gently molds the human mind.

God is no bigot and does not choose His followers the way we do. Through the ages, some of His greatest saints have been lifted from the darkest mud. None need fear to submit to Him for He takes all men where they are and deals with them in love.

Sometimes we get caught off guard. We wander like Eve into forbidden territory. We fail and misrepresent our God. Like David, we may bring dishonor to His name, pain and death to our loved ones, and shame to our own personhood.

But God does not foresake us. His love brings us back, washes away our sins, and cleanses us anew. Often our record is left for others to see as witness to God's methods of mercy. We may rejoice in His everlasting love.

"Now to Him who is able to keep you from falling and to present you before His glorious presence without fault and with great joy, to the only God our Saviour, be glory, majesty, power, and authority, through Jesus Christ our Lord, before all ages now and forevermore. Amen!" (Jude 2:24, 25).

Are Seventh-day Adventists legalists? Do they deny Christ by their teachings regarding obedience to law? Does Adventism, thus, deserve the claim made by some that they are not Christian? I think not, but each reader must settle this question for himself in his own mind through study and prayerful consideration of the Word. The question each one of us must ask: Do I serve Him because I love Him and wish to glorify His name? or because I am afraid of death and the grave? In either event, the service is the same. Only the motive is different. One is love in action. The other is selfishness.

REFERENCE

McMillen, S.I., M.D. None of These Diseases. *Westwood, NJ: Spire Books, Fleming H. Revell Company.*

Thompson, Walter C., M.D. Pearls and Pills. *Amherst, WI: Palmer Publication, Inc., 1988.*

Webster's New Twentieth Century Dictionary. *Second Edition. New York, NY: Simon & Schuster, 1979.*

White, Ellen G. Counsels on Diet and Foods. *Washington, DC: Review and Herald Publishing Company, 1946*

Chapter VI

The Sabbath:
Sign of the Father

The last chapter discussed obedience to law and legalism. According to Adventist belief, the laws God designed and by which the creation of this world was to function are as much in effect now as they were at the time of creation. And while it is impossible for human beings to obey the spirit of the law in their natural state, it is possible when Jesus Christ dwells within them. When Jesus dwells within, there is love, and love is the fulfilling of the great moral law. Few Christians would disagree with this. Furthermore, most Christians acknowledge that lying, stealing, murder, and adultery are sins which are contrary to the principles of Christianity and ought not dominate human existence.

Seventh-day Adventists believe that the fourth of the Ten Commandments (the commandment that describes the Sabbath of Creation) is as much a part of the original law as are the other nine (1, 2). It is as important now for the life, health, and happiness of man as it was when instituted at the end of Creation Week six thousand years ago. Accordingly, people born into the family of God through the "new birth" experience and having the law written upon their hearts by the indwelling presence of Jesus will honor the sanctity of the fourth commandment with the same spirit of love with which they obey and honor the other nine.

1. Genesis 2:3 (NEB): "God blessed the seventh day and made it holy, because on that day he ceased from all the work he had set himself to do."

2. Exodus 20:11 (NEB): "... for in six days the Lord made heaven and earth, the sea, and all that is in them, and on the seventh day he rested. Therefore, the Lord blessed the sabbath day and declared it holy."

This chapter will focus on the Sabbath issue. The evidence upon which Adventist teaching is founded will be studied. Throughout the examination, it will be important to determine whether each bit of the evidence is valid and whether it is being correctly interpreted and applied. The Sabbath plays a very important role in the life and teachings of Adventists. It colors their thinking on many other side issues. It is a major influence in their understanding and teaching regarding end-time events. (To be discussed in later chapters.) It is impossible to understand Adventism without understanding the Adventist definition of Sabbath.

Many Christians believe and teach that the Sabbath

was part of the ancient ceremonial law that was given to the Jews by Moses at Mount Sinai and that this law was taken away and nailed to the cross when Jesus died. It is thereby concluded that the Sabbath must also have been eliminated on the cross.

Is there basis in fact for such an understanding of the Sabbath?

A study of the origin of the word "Sabbath," shows that the word is derived from several roots that when placed together indicate "Sign of the Father," or some similar meaning. Such wording is entirely consistent with the Genesis story relating God's special blessing upon the seventh day (3 through 6).

There are a number of other indicators that suggest that the Sabbath was honored and revered even before the Law was given at Sinai. The Biblical account tells the story in the book of Exodus of how the manna fell in double portions on the sixth day but was not to be found at all on the seventh day. Moreover, on other days of the week, any manna that was kept over from one day to the next spoiled. However, that did not happen to the manna that was preserved on the sixth day for use on the Sabbath (7).

This experience with the manna occurred very shortly after the Jews left Egypt and before the encampment at Mount Sinai. This suggests that the Israelites were aware of the Sabbath before the recording of the Law. If it is true as recorded in Genesis that the Sabbath originated at the end of Creation Week, and if the chronology of the early history of this earth is correct as recorded in the Bible, then a prior knowledge of the Sabbath by the Jews is entirely possible.

According to this record, Adam lived more than 900 years. He and Noah were contemporaries and were very likely acquainted with each other. Noah lived another 350 years after the Flood to become a contemporary with Abraham and probably Isaac. Hence, we see that it was only the span of a few gererations between Creation and the time that Jacob and his family moved to Egypt. How well the knowledge of the Sabbath was preserved in Egypt is not known, but Hebrew texts suggest Sabbath celebrations even there (8).

It is entirely possible, however, that even if the Israelites had lost this knowledge while in Egypt, Moses could well have been reminded of it during his flight into Midian where he lived with other members of his

3. Genesis 2:2, 3 (NEB): "On the sixth day God completed all the work he had been doing; on the seventh day He ceased from all His work. God blessed the seventh day and made it holy . . ."

4. Exodus 31:17 (NEB): "It is a sign forever between me and the Israelites, for in six days the Lord made the heavens and the earth, but on the seventh day he ceased work and refreshed himself."

5. Exodus 23:12 (NEB): "For six days you may do your work, but on the seventh day you shall abstain from work, so that your ox and your ass may rest, and your homeborn slave and the alien may refresh themselves."

6. Exodus 34:21 (NEB): "For six days you shall work, but on the seventh day you shall cease work; even at ploughing time and harvest, you shall cease work."

7. Exodus 16:23, 29 (NEB): "'This,' he answered, 'is what the Lord has said: Tomorrow is a day of sacred rest, a sabbath holy to the Lord.' So bake what you want to bake now, and boil what you want to boil; put aside what remains over and keep it safe till morning . . . The Lord has given you the sabbath, and so he gives you two day's food every sixth day. Let each man stay where he is; no one may stir from his home on the seventh day."

8. Exodus 5:5 (NEB): "Your people already outnumber the native Egyptians; yet you would have them stop working." (i.e., keep Sabbath)

large clan.

This, of course, is not solid confirmation but does point out that the attention given to the Sabbath during the Exodus was not necessarily foreign to the thinking of the people at that time.

Even outside the Biblical account, there is evidence in secular history lending strong support to the existence of the Sabbath in the days before the Jews. One of these evidences may be found in the ancient Chinese pictographs (characters) that make up the written Chinese language. By studying these pictographs, evidence is found suggesting that the ancient Chinese understood the creation and fall of the human race and the sacred nature of the Sabbath the same way as described in the Hebrew record written many centuries later (Nelson and Broadberry, 1979, 55).

> "An old Chinese saying, the returning seventh day, points up to the fact that from very early times, the Chinese have recognized the recurring seven-day cycle which marks the week.

> "Even today the seventh day of the first lunar month of the Chinese year is known as the birthday of mankind; and literally means man's day. Just as it was not the day of man's creation which was to be celebrated, but rather the following day of rest, so the Chinese also celebrate the seventh day as a lingering memorial to God's creative work and the creation of mankind.

> "One cannot help but be impressed with the composition of these ideograms which demonstrate so vividly the ancient history of earth's beginnings, heretofore documented only by the Hebrew writings. But this identical story has also been locked into the Chinese language and preserved for more than 4,000 years for our investigation and study." (Kang, 1979, 55).

To construe from this that the ancient Chinese worshiped on the seventh-day Sabbath may appear presumptuous and without solid evidence to some. But, when put together with other factors, it is interesting to consider the possibility and even the likelihood.

One of these other bits of evidence has to do with the very use of the word "Sabbath" among language and cultural groups around the world. In innumerable cultures, the word for the seventh day of the week is some variation of the English word "Sabbath," e.g., "Sabado" in Spanish, "Sabota" in Polish.

This word in English as in many of these other languages denotes "rest" or "special time." The skeptic may argue that this does not prove that the Sabbath has other than Jewish roots. And, in all honesty, it is possible and indeed probable that the Jews did carry their Sabbath with them wherever in the world they traveled, either willingly or by force. It is less likely, however, that the impact of these Jews upon the nations among whom they lived was so universally positive that their Sabbath was given universal renown. In fact, just the opposite is more reasonable to one who recalls Jewish history and the aversion with which they have often been held by their captors.

If this universal application of Sabbath is not of Jewish origin, one must then seek some other source. Seventh-day Adventists believe that the other source was a direct carryover from Creation.

Another bit of evidence suggesting an ancient origin of the Sabbath is the weekly cycle itself. Why in all the world and in nearly all cultures is the weekly cycle determined in sevens rather than in some other number? Days are reckoned by lightness and darkness. Months are recognized by the lunar cycle; years are reckoned by the seasons. But what determines the seven-day weekly cycle?

Seventh-day Adventists believe that this cycle, too, is a direct consequence of the Creation experience with the designation of every seventh day as the Sabbath. The authority of Scripture defines it to be so.

Joseph Seiss in his book, *The Gospel in the Stars,* makes this interesting observation: "It is generally claimed that the Sabbath and the week of seven days which it marks date back to the beginning of the race to the institution of God himself at the completion of the great creation work ... We find among all the ancient nations—Chaldeans, Persians, Hindus, Chinese, and Egyptians—that the seven days of the week were in universal use; and, what is far more remarkable, each of these nations named the days of the week as we still do after the seven planets numbering the Sun and Moon among them. Hence we say Sun-day, Moon-day, Tuisco or Tuves'-day (Tuisco being the Anglo-Saxon name for Mars), Woden's-day (Woden being the same as Mercury), Thor's-day (Thor being the same as Jupiter), Friga-day (Friga of Freiya being the same as Venus), and lastly Saturn-day, anciently the most sacred of the seven. The order is not that of the distance, velocity, or brilliancy of the orbs named, neither does the first day of the week always coincide among the different nations; but the succession, no matter with which of the days begun, is everywhere the same. It is impossible to suppose this mere accident or chance; and the fact forces the conclusion that the devising and naming of the seven days of the week dates back to some primitive representations of the race" (Seiss, 1986, 22-23).

There are those who suggest that it is fallacious to argue about which day is the Sabbath because in all likelihood the present weekly cycle is not the same as the weekly cycle in ancient times. Hence, the day we now call the Sabbath might very well have been Sunday, Monday, Tuesday, Wednesday, etc. While this is a thought-deserving consideration, evidence attests to the fact that there has been no alteration in the seven-day cycle for as far back into human history as there is any record.

Jesus set us an example of Sabbath worship, and the historical record is very clear that there has been no change in the weekly cycle since He walked on earth. (For further study, see *The Sabbath in Scripture and History* and *From Sabbath to Sunday.)*

Christianity has its roots in Judaism. The Sabbath was a very prominent feature of their religion and one that often aided in distinguishing them from their pagan neighbors (9). Over and over again as one studies the Old Testament Scriptures, he notes that Israel's success as a nation very closely corresponded to the diligence with which they honored the Sabbath (10, 11).

Actually, their reverence for the Sabbath very closely paralleled their loyalty to the true God in preference to the pagan gods and vice versa. This suggests that there was something about the Sabbath that served to protect them from the worship of false Gods as well.

Centuries later, it was the custom of Jesus to worship on the Sabbath Day (12). True, His form of worship was an abomination to the straightlaced and legalistic Jews (13). Nonetheless, the sanctity of the day remains by His example.

Following Christ's crucifixion, the early Christian church continued to worship on the seventh-day Sab-

9. *Exodus 31:13 (NEB):* "Speak to the Israelites, you yourself, and say to them: Above all you shall observe my sabbath, for the sabbath is a sign between me and you in every generation that you may know that I am the Lord who hallows you."

10. *Ezekiel 20:13, 14 (NEB):* "But the Israelites rebelled against me in the wilderness; they did not conform to my statutes, they rejected my laws, though by keeping them men might have life, and they utterly desecrated my sabbaths. So again I thought to pour out my wrath on them in the wilderness to destroy them. I acted for the honour of my name, that it might not be profaned in the sight of the nations who had seen me bring them out."

11. *Isaiah 56:2, 6, 7 (NEB):* "Happy is the man who follows these precepts, happy the mortal who holds them fast, who keeps the sabbath undefiled, who refrains from all wrong-doing! ... So too with the foreigners who give their allegiance to me, the Lord, to minister to me and love my name and to become my servants, all who keep the sabbath undefiled and hold fast to my covenant: them will I bring to my holy hill and give them joy in my house of prayer. Their offerings and sacrifices shall be acceptable on my altar; for my house shall be called a house of prayer for all nations."

12. *Luke 4:16 (NEB):* "So he came to Nazareth, where he had been brought up, and went to synagogue on the Sabbath day as he regularly did."

13. *John 5:8-10, 16 (NEB):* "Jesus answered, 'Rise to your feet, take up your bed, and walk.' The man recovered instantly, took up his stretcher, and began to walk. That day was a Sabbath. So the Jews said to the man who had been cured, 'It is the Sabbath. You are not allowed to carry your bed on the Sabbath.' ... It was works of this kind done on the Sabbath that stirred the Jews to persecute Jesus."

bath. There is no reference in the New Testament that they did otherwise (14, 15). There are references of Christians gathering on the first day of the week but no designation that this was in honor of a change of the day of worship.

The Apostle John received his vision of Revelation on the Lord's Day. Many Christians have claimed that this reference is to the first day of the week and indicate that he acknowledged it as the new Christian day of worship. However, early church history does not really allow one to confirm this argument (Bacchiocchi, 1977, 111-131).

It is true that the early Christians were often viewed as a sect of Judaism and were opposed by both Jews and Gentiles. One of the means that took root quite early in the Christian church to alter this reputation was to gather for worship on the first day of the week. Since the resurrection was such a powerful selling factor in confirming the true identity of Jesus as God in showing His power over death, it would have been quite natural for early Christians to be drawn to this day for celebration. There is nothing in either Scripture or secular history that convincingly suggests that any of the apostles reverenced any other day of the week than the seventh-day Sabbath, however.

In fact, the historical record indicates that as the early apostles under the power of Pentecost carried the Gospel to the world, they took the knowledge of the Sabbath with them (Wilkinson, 1944).

Eventually as the anti-Judaistic element gained in strength, those who persisted in their worship of God on the seventh day became known as Judaisers, Sabbatarians, and Insabbati. For their persistence, they were often persecuted. To avoid persecution, many of the early Christians honored other holy days, de-emphasizing the seventh-day Sabbath and the Roman persecution that often accompanied it.

The point is that the Bible fails to indicate a change in the sanctity of the Sabbath to Sunday. Church history also fails to identify such an event. What is noted in history, however, is that although there was no declaration by God of a change in worship from one day to the other, Sunday developed an increasingly prominent role in the development of the Christian church, and especially in the Roman arm of the church.

While devout Christians in all parts of the world

followed the early Apostolic example of Sabbath worship, Sunday worship came to dominate that portion of the church which was subject to Rome. As the Bishop of Rome became ever more powerful relative to the other regional bishops, Sunday worship also saw increasing support. Eventually, by the time of Constantine, the church had gained the support of the state and acting together the day of worship of the Christian church was essentially changed from the seventh to the first day of the week.

To this day the Catholic church acknowledges its role in making this change. It claims the authority to make such change based upon the statement made by Jesus to Peter interpreting the statement to indicate that Peter and his successors would be the rock upon whom the church would be built (Matthew 16:18, 19).

While this statement of Jesus is open to other interpretations, it is true that the Roman Catholic Church used it as authority whereby to become a very powerful force in both the religious and secular world, dominating the Western world for many centuries (Note: Church historians date the interpretation of this beginning in about the fourth century. It was not interpreted like this in the beginning.)

Sunday worship was a very prominent mark of the Catholic Church's authority and has remained so to the present time. The question is not whether or not the church has changed the day when most Christians worship from the seventh to the first day of the week, but whether or not this change originated in heaven with the Creator or on earth by some authority other than the God of heaven.

Seventh-day Adventists adopt the position of those Christians who through the centuries have clung to the teachings of the Holy Scriptures, including the Sabbath, rather than compromise with the pagan world around them in an effort to either convert them or to avoid persecution.

Although the Seventh-day Adventist Church did not arise as an identifiable entity until the mid-nineteenth century, it identifies its heritage among Sabbath-keeping Christians in all lands throughout the Christian era. Ample records indicate the existence of Sabbath-keeping Christians in various parts of the world throughout the Christian era. (See *Truth Triumphant* and *The Sabbath of God through the Centuries.*)

Adventists find it impossible to interpret Jesus'

16. *Ephesians 2:20 (NEB):*
"You are built upon the foundation laid by the apostles and prophets, and Christ Jesus himself is the foundation-stone."

17. *Acts 4:11 (NEB):*
"This Jesus is the stone rejected by the builders which has become the keystone—and you are the builders."

18. *I Peter 2:6 (NEB):*
"For it stands written: 'I lay in Zion a choice corner-stone of great worth. The man who has faith in it will not be put to shame.'"

19. *I Corinthians 3:11 (NEB): "Let each take care how he builds. There can be no other foundation beyond that which is already laid; I mean Jesus Christ himself."*

20. *Matthew 7:16 (NEB): "You will recognize them by the fruits they bear. Can grapes be picked from briars, or figs from thistles?"*

21. *Exodus 34:6, 7 (NEB): "Then the Lord passed in front of him and called aloud, 'Jehovah, the Lord, a god compassionate and gracious, long-suffering, ever constant and true, maintaining constancy to thousands, forgiving iniquity, rebellion, and sin, and not sweeping the guilty clean away; but one who punishes sons and grandsons to the third and fourth generation for the iniquity of their fathers!'"*

22. *Galatians 3:11 (NEB): "It is evident that no one is ever justified before God in terms of law; because we read, 'He shall gain life who is justified through faith.'"*

23. *Galatians 2:20 (NEB): "I have been crucified with Christ: the life I now live is not my life, but the life which Christ lives in me; and my present bodily life is lived by faith in the Son of God, who loved me and gave himself up for me."*

words to Peter in the same way that the Roman Catholic Church interprets them. Jesus Christ has always been the rock upon whom the church was built and has remained so to the present time (16 through 19).

The Holy Scriptures identify guidelines by which a prophet or a spokesman for God may be identified.

One of these guidelines states that, "Ye shall know them by their fruits" (20). The record of fruit-bearing by the Roman Catholic Church through the centuries has fallen short of meeting this criteria. Adventists argue that it is inconceivable to believe that one who claims to be the voice and authority of Christ could govern by such drastically different principles—that one who came to this world to offer Himself in self-sacrificing love to save the world could sanction the practices of an organization that would persecute and kill to gain compliance. The historical record is clear (Hroch and Skybova, 1988, 11-12).

Thus, the Seventh-day Adventist position remains that the change of the sabbath from the seventh to the first day of the week was not accomplished upon the authority of God, and that the seventh-day Sabbath maintains all of the sanctity that it was given at the end of the Creation week.

There are those, both Christian and non-Christian, who suggest that the day which one chooses to worship his God is not important so long as one does worship one's God. If God is indeed a patient, kind, loving, long-suffering, and prayer-answering God as He describes Himself, then certainly He must be sufficiently malleable to meet us on whichever day we decide to worship (21).

Paul's letter to the Galatians is often interpreted to suggest just such an argument. Adventists believe that this argument misses the gist of what Paul is trying to get across. Here, as elsewhere, he is preaching about the importance of the life in which Christ lives, where obedience is the fruit or natural result of the law written on the heart as an expression of love. He is not suggesting that God no longer has laws by which to govern His universe (22 through 27).

Adventists believe that God as the Creator has the authority to command our worship on the day of His choosing. Any change ought properly to come from Him (28 through 30). The command regarding Sabbath holiness was not an arbitrary command given without purpose. Rather, like the other nine commandments, it was an instrument facilitating harmony in God's universe. The Sabbath was designated as holy time and remains forever as holy time. The blessing is for all who will join in its celebration. It is a time to spend in fellowship with God, a time to refocus priorities, to break away from the stress and strain of the workaday world. It is a memorial, a monument of time, set apart to remind us of our roots. To disregard the sabbath command is paramount to ignoring His love and disregarding His authority.

The following quotation taken from a recent article in the *Adventist Review* notes some of the benefits of Sabbath celebration:

> "The meaning of the Sabbath is the truth that God is love—creative, forgiving, redeeming, transforming love. Let me try to explain how this works out in the experience of the Sabbath.

> "The Sabbath experience means that God's love is the center of our existence. It is a recognition of God as Creator, the ultimate source of everything we have or are. No person is self-made, however hard one works to succeed.

> "The Sabbath also reminds us that the meaning of our lives depends not on what we achieve but on the fact that we are loved and accepted, forgiven and redeemed by God Himself.

> "The Sabbath means rest in Christ. 'Come to me,' He said, 'all you who are weary and burdened, and I will give you rest.' (Matthew 11:28).

> "Every Sabbath comes as a gift. It is not a reward either for six days of hard work or for diligent preparation.

> "The Sabbath can be for us an experience of eternity in time. The Sabbath experience is an awareness of the presence of God—an experience of Immanuel, 'God is with us.'

> "The Sabbath provides time for worship. It stops every day activity as much as possible so that we can concentrate on our relationship with God. It gives us time to reaffirm our commitment to our supreme values and to try to understand their implications in our lives.

24. *Galatians 5:13 (NEB):* "You, my friends, were called to be free men; only do not turn your freedom into license for your lower nature, but be servants to one another in love."

25. *Galatians 5:18 (NEB):* "But if you are led by the Spirit, you are not under law."

26. *Galatians 5:22, 23 (NEB):* "But the harvest of the Spirit is love, joy, peace, patience, kindness, goodness, fidelity, gentleness, and self-control. There is no law dealing with such things as these."

27. *Galatians 2:16 (NEB):* "But we know that no man is ever justified by doing what the law demands, but only through faith in Christ Jesus; so we too have put our faith in Jesus Christ, in order that we might be justified through this faith, and not through deeds dictated by law; for by such deeds, Scripture says, no mortal man shall be justified."

28. *Luke 6:5 (NEB):* "He also said, 'The Son of Man is sovereign even over the Sabbath.'"

29. *Ephesians 1:22 (NEB):* "He put everything in subjection beneath his feet."

30. *I Peter 3:22 (NEB):* "It brings salvation through the resurrection of Jesus Christ, who entered heaven after receiving the submission of angelic authorities and powers, and is now at the right hand of God."

"God and our basic values are never absent from our lives or consciousness, but most of the week other things demand our primary attention. The Sabbath gives us time to direct our attention to eternal realities.

"It is something like being in love. When you are at work, you should be thinking primarily about your work, although the one you love is never completely absent from your consciousness. But you need and want occasions when your attention is focused primarily on the one you love. Time for worship is to religious life what time for intimacy is to love" (Guy, 1987).

Obedience to the fourth commandment like all of the rest of God's law may be done legalistically and the Sabbath day may be made a day of burden and pain. Acknowledging this danger, Adventists believe the benefit of true Sabbath celebration far out weighs any potential abuse by legalism. And should such legalistic obedience occur among some of its members, does this justify the denunciation so often given as the reason to classify the organization as a "cult"?

REFERENCE

Bacchiocchi, Samuele, From Sabbath to Sunday. Rome: The Pontifical Gregorian University Press, 1977.

Coltheart, J.F. The Sabbath of God Through the Centuries. Payson, AZ: Leaves of Autumn Books, Inc., 1954.

Guy, Fritz. "Eternity in Time," Adventist Review. May 28, 1987. Washington, DC: Review and Herald Publishing Association.

Haynes, Carlyle B. From Sabbath to Sunday. Washington, DC: Review and Herald Publishing Association, 1928.

Hroch, Miroslav and Anna Skybova. Ecclesia Militans The Inquisition. Dorset Press, 1988.

Kang, C.H. and Ethel R. Nelson. The Discovery of Genesis. St. Louis: Concordia Publishing House, 1979.

Seiss, Joseph A. The Gospel in the Stars. Grand Rapids, MI: Kregel Publications, 1982.

Nelson, Ethel R. and Richard E. Broadberry. Mysteries Confucius Couldn't Solve. South Lancaster, MA: Read Books Publishing, 1986.

Strand, Kenneth A. The Sabbath in Scripture and History. Washington, DC: Review and Herald Publishing Association, 1982.

Wilkinson, Benjamin G. Truth Triumphant. Mountain View, CA: Pacific Press Publishing Association, 1944.

Chapter VII

Modern-day Prophet

Jesus described the events that will precede His return to this world at the end of time in this way: "Many will fall from their faith; they will betray one another and hate one another. Many false prophets will arise, and mislead many . . ." (Matthew 24:10, 11).

Seventh-day Adventists believe that Ellen Gould Harmon White was a prophetess of God. They believe that she was a messenger through whom God gave direction to the Advent movement as it prepared to proclaim the last warning message of God's mercy to the world dying in sin. Adventists are convinced that Ellen White met all of the criteria outlined in the Bible with which to test a true prophet. Her writings have certainly played a major role in Adventist thought and action. Most other Christians would classify her as a false prophet and echo the warning of Jesus to beware.

One of the characteristics of a cult is the fact that it has a code of belief and behavior that lies outside of the Holy Scriptures and replaces or pre-empts the teaching of Scripture. Some critics contend that Adventists exalt Ellen White above Scripture and, therefore, deserve to be designated as a cult. Is this true? Does Ellen White meet the criteria of false prophets that Jesus warned against?

It was the night before the Crucifixion. Jesus knew that His time to leave this world had come. Even His disciples sensed that things were about to change, although they had not been able to understand some of the strange things Jesus had tried to tell them. To calm their anxiety and to prepare them to carry on the work that He had begun, He told them that when He was gone, He would send another, the Holy Spirit, who could be everywhere at once to guide them in their work. Because the Holy Spirit would not be limited by time and space as Jesus was, Jesus could assure them that they would do even greater works than He had done. The Spirit would continue Jesus' work of convicting the world of sin and imploring it to repent and follow Him (1 through 3).

The gifts to be imparted to human beings through the ministry of the Holy Spirit were first manifested at the time of Pentecost a few days after Jesus' last appearance to them. These gifts were responsible for

1. John 14:12 (NEB): "In truth, in very truth, I tell you, he who has faith in me will do what I am doing; and he will do greater things still because I am going to the Father."

2. John 16:8, 9 (NEB): "When he comes, he will confute the world, and show where wrong and right and judgment lie. He will convict them of wrong, by their refusal to believe in me."

3. Acts 2:17,18 (NEB): "No, this is what the prophet spoke of: God says, 'This will happen in the last days: I will pour out upon everyone a portion of my spirit; and your sons and daughters shall prophesy; your young men shall see visions, and your old men shall dream dreams. Yes, I will endue even my slaves, both men and women, with a portion of my spirit, and they shall prophesy.'"

4. I Corinthians 12:4-11 (NEB): "There are varieties of gifts, but the same Spirit. There are varieties of service, but the same Lord. There are many forms of work, but all of them in all men, are the work of the same God. In each of us the Spirit is manifested in one particular way, for some useful purpose. One man, through the Spirit, has the gift of wise speech, while another, by the power of the same Spirit, can put the deepest knowledge into words. Another, by the same Spirit, is granted faith; another, by the one Spirit, gifts of healing, and another miraculous powers; another has the gift of prophecy, and another ability to distinguish true spirits from false; yet another has the gift of ecstatic utterance of different kinds, and another the ability to interpret it. But all these gifts are the work of one and the same Spirit, distributing them separately to each individual at will."

5. II Chronicles 20:20 (NEB): "So they rose early in the morning and went out to the wilderness of Tekoa; and, as they were starting, Jehoshaphat took his stand and said, 'Hear me, O Judah and inhabitants of Jerusalem: hold firmly to your faith in the Lord your God and you will be upheld; have faith in his prophets and you will prosper.'"

6. Amos 3:7 (NEB): "For the Lord God does nothing without giving to his servants the prophets knowledge of his plans."

7. Daniel 2:22 (NEB): "He reveals deep mysteries; he knows what lies in darkness, and light has its dwelling with him."

8. Joel 2:28 (NIV): "And afterward, I will pour out my Spirit on all people. Your sons and daughters will prophesy, your old men will dream dreams, your young men will see visions."

the rapid spread of the Good News of Jesus' atoning sacrifice and resurrection. Paul in his letters to the Romans and the believers at Corinth listed these gifts and indicated that these were the means by which the work of Christ on earth would be accomplished (4).

Seventh-day Adventists believe that these gifts of the Holy Spirit are real and that they represent supernatural experiences that occur in persons chosen by God in response to the corporate need of His followers. The gifts are given at times when God's people are sincere in their willingness to be used by God for the salvation of their fellow men (5).

Among these gifts is the gift of prophecy (6, 7). Always in history God has had His messengers through whom He has spoken to the human race. These voices have been most audible at those points in history that have been most critical to the accomplishment of His purpose and overall plan.

There is nothing written in the Bible to indicate that God would no longer speak to our race through the human agent of a prophet. In fact, as already cited, the gifts of the spirit include that of prophecy. Adventists believe that if ever there were a time in history when it was important for God to speak to human beings in their own language, it must be now as the end of the world approaches. Accordingly, Seventh-day Adventists believe that the prophetic gift has appeared to men at this time (8).

The return of Christ focused upon two determining characteristics of the chosen ones: 1) their obedience to the commandments and, 2) their witness to the testimony of Jesus (9, 10). He later indicates that "the testimony of Jesus" is the spirit of prophecy (11). Adventists interpret these writings of John in the Book of Revelation to indicate that the prophetic gift will be one of the identifying characteristics of God's people in the last days.

Ellen G. White was a young lady at the time of the Great Disappointment of 1844. She experienced the intense disappointment along with all of the rest. With them she joined in the search for understanding.

Soon God began to reveal to her in vision and in dreams such things as the nature of the conflict between good and evil, the significance of the present time and the means by which the world might be prepared for the coming of Christ.

To a large extent the world has rejected Ellen White

as a prophet and as a spokesperson for God. Only among Adventist people have her messages been heeded and promoted, although Adventists believe they were intended for the whole world.

The Scriptures identify a number of tests whereby a supposed messenger prophet may be evaluated (12). Should the messenger meet the requirements of these tests and still be rejected and labeled as false, it is tantamount to rejection of the Holy Spirit Himself. For, as has been noted, the gifts of the Spirit are the very work of the Spirit in the human agent (13 through 15).

Jesus Himself has declared that there is only one sin that is unforgivable and that is the sin against the Holy Spirit; i.e., rejection of the Spirit's efforts to work out our salvation, whatever form those efforts take. If God has indeed spoken through a modern day prophet, it is a very dangerous thing to ignore either the messenger or her message (16).

There are several means by which the Holy Scriptures instructs its readers to test the validity of a message or a messenger claiming to be from God. One such test compares the message under investigation with other inspired writings (the Holy Scriptures). If in any way the message in question clearly contradicts the Scriptures, we can safely acknowledge it as false (18). There is a word of caution here because Satan's most successful deceptions are often counterfeits of the truth. As is so often the case with counterfeits, very thorough study is necessary to identify them. Another identifying characteristic of a true message, especially if it be predictive or prophetic in nature, is whether or not the prediction comes to pass (19). (The Bible cites multiple examples of an exception to this rule where predictions forecasting doom did not come to pass even though given by true prophets. It is interesting that all of these examples were prophecies containing the little word "if" indicating their conditional nature. Ninevah repented and Jonah's prophecy was not fulfilled. Other examples might be mentioned.)

A third measure verifying the origin of a message is that of the fruits that it bears. Jesus said, "By their fruits ye shall know them" (20). Everyone is familiar with beautiful apples that have worms inside. It is mandatory to remember that when studying the fruits, a superficial look is insufficient. One must rather look at both the short-term and long-term effects, the ripple

9. *Revelation 12:17 (NEB):* "At this the dragon grew furious with the woman, and went off to wage war on the rest of her offspring, that is, on those who keep God's commandments and maintain their testimony to Jesus."

10. *Revelation 14:1, 12 (NEB):* "Then I looked, and on Mount Zion stood the Lamb, and with him were a hundred and forty-four thousand who had his name and the name of his Father written on their foreheads ... This is where the fortitude of God's people has its place—in keeping God's commands and remaining loyal to Jesus."

11. *Revelation 19:10 (KJV):* "And I fell at his feet to worship him. And he said unto me, See thou do it not: I am thy fellow servant, and of thy brethren that have the testimony of Jesus: worship God: for the testimony of Jesus is the spirit of prophecy."

12. *I John 4:1 (NEB):* "But do not trust any and every spirit, my friends; test the spirits, to see whether they are from God, for among those who have gone out into the world there are many prophets falsely inspired."

13. *I Thessalonians 5:19-22 (NEB):* "Do not stifle inspiration, and do not despise prophetic utterances, but bring them all to the test and then keep what is good in them and avoid the bad of whatever kind."

14. *Ephesians 4:30 (NEB):* "And do not grieve the Holy Spirit of God, for that Spirit is the seal with which you were marked for the day of our final liberation."

15. *II Peter 1:21 (NEB):* "For it was not through any human whim that men prophesied of old; men they were, but, impelled by the Holy Spirit, they spoke the words of God."

16. Matthew 12:31 (NEB): "And so I tell you this: no sin, no slander, is beyond forgiveness for men, except slander spoken against the Spirit, and that will not be forgiven."

17. Matthew 24:24 (NEB): "Impostors will come claiming to be messiahs or prophets, and they will produce great signs and wonders to mislead even God's chosen, if such a thing were possible."

18. Isaiah 8:20 (KJV): "To the law and to the testimony: if they speak not according to this word, it is because there is no light in them."

19. Jeremiah 28:9 (NEB): "If a prophet foretells prosperity, when his words come true it will be known that the Lord has sent him."

20. Matthew 7:15-22 (NIV): "Watch out for false prophets. They come to you in sheep's clothing, but inwardly they are ferocious wolves. By their fruit you will recognize them. Do people pick grapes from thornbushes, or figs from thistles? Likewise every good tree bears good fruit, but a bad tree bears bad fruit. A good tree cannot bear bad fruit and a bad tree cannot bear good fruit. Every tree that does not bear good fruit is cut down and thrown into the fire. Thus, by their fruit you will recognize them. Not everyone who says to me, 'Lord, Lord,' will enter the kingdom of heaven, but only he who does the will of my Father who is in heaven. Many will say to me on that day, 'Lord, Lord, did we not prophesy in your name, and in your name drive out demons and perform many miracles?'"

21. I John 4:2, 3 (NEB): "This is how we may recognize the Spirit of God: every spirit which acknowledges that Jesus Christ has come in the flesh is from God, and every spir-it which does not thus acknowledge Jesus is not from God. This is what is meant by 'Antichrist'; you have been told that he was to come, and here he is, in the world already!"

effects and ramifications of any given message. But if the message bears the tests and in all things gives glory to God we may know its true source.

A fourth test looks at the message and the messenger to determine if they are focused upon Christ as the Savior of the world and bearer of our sins. Many false prophets and false teachers claim to believe in Christ, but the fruits of their lives are contrary to the very things that He taught and fought for and for which He died. A true prophet or spokesman for God will certainly both live as well as speak the truth about Jesus (17) (21, 22).

Using these guidelines, it should be possible to evaluate any message or any messenger to determine whether they are speaking according to the Holy Spirit or not. In addition to these, however, at least on some occasions, prophets while in vision exhibited supernatural phenomena. It is recorded that while in vision some did not breathe, some had eyes opened but did not see, many had supernatural strength or supernatural weakness (23). When these phenomena are present, they may be another means of confirming the validity of the messenger. Here one must be careful, however, again because of the ability of Satan to perform miracles himself and demonstrate supernatural phenomena.

Seventh-day Adventists have scrutinized Ellen White according to the above mentioned criteria both from a friendly and a hostile viewpoint. In addition, attorneys, theologians, and common folk of other faiths have at other times thoroughly studied the message of Ellen White. As a consequence, there are both believers and non-believers. What is interesting is that it is difficult to find fault with the message when measured by the above criteria. Books such as *Steps to Christ, Thoughts from the Mount of Blessings, Ministry of Healing, Education, Christ Object Lessons,* or *Desire of Ages* all lift up Christ and encourage dedication of the life to His service. In fact, the record confirms that the messenger herself lived a very godly and Christlike life. But Ellen White bore a message of rebuke to the resisting person. Her message calls for complete surrender to the high calling of God and magnifies the beauty of Christ and one's dependence upon Him for one's salvation. Messages of this sort are not popular and Adventists believe they have undoubtedly contributed to the rejection of both the message

56

and the messenger.

While Adventists deny that Ellen White in any way contradicts the Bible, it is true that some of the visions which are recorded in her writings carry one beyond the sometimes brief descriptions of Scripture with much greater detail and timeliness to the present day. One example of this was revealed to this author during a recent tour of the Holy Land. While our group was visiting various sites, the bus driver stayed with the bus and read Ellen White's book, *Desire of Ages,* a well-known commentary on the life of Christ.

One day upon returning from our visit in the region of Gadera, this Israeli bus driver made an interesting, unsolicited comment to the effect that whoever wrote this book must have either been inspired or have lived in Israel herself for in no other way could she have been so accurate about details.

Other areas of Ellen White's writing reach out beyond Scripture to deal with healthful living, true education, Last Day events, etc.

Adventists find it difficult to understand the criticism often voiced regarding the very concept of modern-day prophets. The Bible clearly identifies prophecy as one of the gifts by which the Holy Spirit blesses the church. It is equally difficult to understand why Ellen White's female gender causes such reaction. According to the Bible, she is not the first such woman. They find it even more difficult to understand rejection of her by those who have not thoroughly applied the tests that the Scriptures outline whereby to test the prophets.

There are some who would attribute the experience of Ellen White to a seizure disorder, to a mental disturbance, or to some other illness. Some anthropologists would attribute her message and the movement of which she was a part to a natural reaction of social trauma that arose out of the Great Disappointment of 1844. They note that such experience frequently create religious enthusiasm and eccentricity. But, Adventists would ask, how often in this world are human beings forced to lie on their backs in personal trauma before they will yield to the beckoning calls of the Holy Spirit and look up? May societal trauma not serve a similar outcome?

That there was such a relationship between the Great Disappointment of 1844 and the subsequent development of the Advent movement should not seem

22. Deuteronomy 13:1-3 (NEB): "When a prophet or dreamer appears among you and offers you a sign or a portent and calls on you to follow other gods whom you have not known and worship them, even if the sign or portent should come true, do not listen to the words of that prophet or that dreamer. God is testing you through him to discover whether you love the Lord your God with all your heart and soul."

23. Daniel 10:8, 9, 17 (NEB): "And I was left alone gazing at this great vision. But my strength left me; I became a sorry figure of a man, and retained no strength. I heard the sound of his words and, when I did so, I fell prone on the ground in a trance ... How can my lord's servant presume to talk with such as my lord, since my strength has failed me and no breath is left in me?"

strange nor should it serve to prove that God was not leading the movement. Rather, it is wise to recall that all of God's dealings with human beings occur according to His timetable and can only occur when the stage has been set and the actors are ready.

"My friends, test the spirits, to see whether they are from God" (I John 4:1).

Some of Ellen White's impact on the Church and the world will be the topic of later chapters. The reader will need to consider as he reads whether or not each impact is positive or negative. Reason must dictate that White is either a true prophet or she is a false one; Biblical teaching does not allow one to be both. If she is indeed proven false by the evidence, Adventism must certainly qualify as a cult. If, on the other hand, she should pass the tests for a true prophet of God, what then?

REFERENCE

White, Ellen G. Christ's Object Lessons. Mountain View, CA: Pacific Press Publishing Association.

White, Ellen G. The Desire of Ages. Mountain View, CA: Pacific Press Publishing Association, 1940.

White, Ellen G. Education. Mountain View, CA: Pacific Press Publishing Association, 1952.

White, Ellen G. The Ministry of Healing. Mountain View, CA: Pacific Press Publishing Association.

White, Ellen G. Steps to Christ. Mountain View, CA: Pacific Press Publishing Association

White, Ellen G. Thoughts from the Mount of Blessing. Washington, DC: Review and Herald Publishing Association, 1956.

Chapter VIII

The Health Message

In many circles, Adventists are known because of their health practices and dietary restrictions. Critics sometimes refer to Paul's letters to Timothy and the believers in Corinth and Colossae to disclaim their teaching (1 through 3). They suggest thereby that the health doctrine makes Adventists legalistic. (As mentioned elsewhere, Adventists would distinguish between obedience to law for its inherent value as contrasted with that obedience that is done to gain merit. For the one who loves his Lord, obedience is the natural outcome of that love and tends to give glory to the creator. On the other hand, obedience used to gain merit is pure selfishness and is contrary to God's purpose for us.) Now, if the teachings regarding health and lifestyle practices as taught by Adventists are scientifically correct, and if they are practiced in response to love, does such a practice bring dishonor to God and to Christianity?

Following the Great Disappointment of 1844 the undaunted believers bore a heavy conviction that the Advent movement was directed by God and had been raised up to prepare the world for His soon return. Although few in number, they accepted their calling and set out to share their new found hope with the world. There was a problem. Their task of preaching to a disappointed, disbelieving, and hardened world was seriously hampered by the poor health of these early believers of the Advent.

But God had a plan that must not be curtailed. Here in man's frailty, God found opportunity. It was in this setting of struggle and poor health that Ellen White was given her first vision regarding health reform. She was shown the principles of healthful living and the benefits that might be expected by lifestyle change. In subsequent visions, details of this health message were filled in as a comprehensive health care ministry emerged and developed within the Advent movement.

What could be so important to God about people's lifestyle practices and health habits as to cause Him through the Holy Spirit to use this as a major function of the prophetic gift? The Scriptures give some clues.

At the time of the Exodus, God had a similar prob-

1. *I Timothy 4:1-4 (KJV):* "Now the Spirit speaketh expressly, that in the latter times some shall depart from the faith, giving heed to seducing spirits, and doctrines of devils; Speaking lies in hypocrisy; having their conscience seared with a hot iron; Forbidding to marry, and commanding to abstain from meats, which God hath created to be received with thanksgiving of them which believe and know the truth. For every creature of God is good, and nothing to be refused, if it be received with thanksgiving; For it is sanctified by the word of God and prayer."

2. *Colossians 2:16 (KJV):* "Let no man therefore judge you in meat, or in drink, or in respect of a holy day, or of the new moon, or of the sabbath days."

3. *I Corinthians 10:25 (KJV):* "Whatsoever is sold in the shambles, that eat, asking no question for conscience sake."

59

4. *Deuteronomy 6:1-3 (NEB): "These are the commandments, statutes, and laws which the Lord your God commanded me to teach you to observe in the land into which you are passing to occupy it, a land flowing with milk and honey, so that you may fear the Lord your God and keep all his statutes and commandments which I am giving you, both you, your sons, and your descendants all your lives, and so that you may live long. If you listen, O Israel, and are careful to observe them, you will prosper and increase greatly as the Lord the God of your fathers promised you."*

5. *Deuteronomy 28:1, 2 (NEB): "If you will obey the Lord your god by diligently observing all his commandments which I lay upon you this day, then the Lord your God will raise you high above all nations of the earth, and all these blessings shall come to you and light upon you, because you obey the Lord your God."*

6. *Deuteronomy 7:12-15 (NEB): "If you listen to these laws and are careful to observe them, then the Lord your God will observe the sworn covenant he made with your forefathers and will keep faith with you. He will love you, bless you and cause you to increase. He will bless the fruit of your body and the fruit of your land, your corn and new wine and oil, the offspring of your herds, and of your lambing flocks, in the land which he swore to your forefathers to give you. You shall be blessed above every other nation; neither among your people nor among your cattle shall there be impotent male or barren female. The Lord will take away all sickness from you; he will not bring you any of the foul diseases of Egypt which you know so well, but will bring them upon all your enemies."*

7. *Exodus 15:26 (NEB): "It was there that the Lord laid down a precept and rule of life, there he put them to the test. He said, 'If only you will*

lem. He had a world that He loved, dying in sin. Indeed, His very chosen ones—the descendants of Abraham, Isaac, and Jacob—had reached the depths of human existence while under the slavery of the Egyptians. Merely taking them out of Egypt would not of itself make them a healthy and holy nation whereby the light of His truth might radiate out to flood the world. No, before they could serve such a noble function, they must themselves be restored to fullness of life, physically, mentally, and spiritually. To accomplish this, to develop a people who would be an example to the world, a nation enjoying life to its fullest capacity that would attract the world to a knowledge of God and of His love and concern, God gave the law now known as the Law of Moses. Contained within this law there was instruction regarding all aspects of life, not the least of which were regulations concerning healthful lifestyle practices (4 through 7). In fact, God told them that he was placing them at the crossroads of the nations to share their blessings with them. Perchance others seeing the true God which Israel worshipped would also turn to Him for healing (8 through 14).

Adventists perceive a similar role for their health-related doctrine.

With this introduction, it is time to look at the message and examine its application to see if its function is fulfilling God's purpose of tipping the scales and restoring a people (a remnant) from among the race of men.

The message in essence is this: Begin with the messenger. Instruct him upon the principles of health, and let him experience the healing virtues. Then, convinced by experience of its benefits, send him out onto the inhabitants of the hurting world to bind up their wounds, to heal their diseases, and to teach them the ways of health and happiness. Having accomplished this he may then, after the example of the Master, invite them to follow Jesus to full restoration.

Health could only reach optimum status in a setting where the laws governing it were known and observed. Though simple, these laws would be contrary to human nature. Compliance would require effort and often painful change. Ellen White taught that it is indulgence of the senses and greed for gain that lie at the root of much of our modern day suffering—physical as well as mental and spiritual. Nature's laws identify eight areas of emphasis that give healing. They begin with:

1. A diet that is well-balanced, composed of a wide variety of natural foods with a minimal amount of processing, prepared so as to have both visual and taste appeal. The original diet as given to Adam and Eve was composed of the plants of the earth, their fruit, and seeds. Animal products were not a part of the original diet and Adventists believe they are not now part of an ideal diet either (15). Many Adventists for this reason are vegetarian or near-vegetarian.

2. The human body is designed to function in an environment of fresh air and pure water. Individually we have limited control of the air we breathe, but can often avoid contamination of tobacco smoke and other pollutants.

3. Water is an ideal thirst quencher and has great value both for internal and external use. Its use is encouraged in disease prevention and treatment.

4. Exercise is recognized the world over as an essential component to health. Yet, of all times in world history, this society is undoubtedly the least exercised, a fact attributable to modern means of transportation and communication. It is mandatory that we plan our exercise to compensate for these "modern miracles" if we wish to continue to use them.

5. The bodies of men were tuned to operate by carefully programmed rhythms or cycles. Rest, relaxation, and sleep are all essentials to health and are most beneficial when utilized within the framework of the cycles established within our being.

6. The world is to a large extent governed by the light and heat from the sun. This, too, impacts upon health. The sun helps control body rhythms, impacts upon the body's defense mechanisms, and effects such subtle things as moods. Proper utilization of the light of the sun is also part of healthful living.

7. While the world is blessed with so many beautiful things that when intelligently utilized give blessings, many of these same potentially beneficial things can be destructive when abused. Thus, a healthful lifestyle mandates that intellect dominate being and control the sensual experience for optimal health, avoiding altogether harmful things, and using good things in moderation.

8. Unfortunately, human nature is messed up by sin

obey the Lord your god, if you will do what is right in his eyes, if you will listen to his commands and keep all his statutes, then I will never bring upon you any of the sufferings which I brought on the Egyptians; for I the Lord am your healer.'"

8. Isaiah 49:6 (NIV): "He says: 'It is too small a thing for you to be my servant to restore the tribes of Jacob and bring back those of Israel I have kept. I will also make you a light for the Gentiles, that you may bring my salvation to the ends of the earth.'"

9. Hosea 2:23 (NIV): "I will plant her for myself in the land; I will show my love to the one I called 'Not my loved one.' I will say to those called 'Not my people,' 'You are my people;' and they will say, 'You are my God.'"

10. Isaish 45:22 (NIV): "Turn to me and be saved, all you ends of the earth; for I am God, and there is no other."

11. II Corinthians 5:18 (NEB): "From first to last this has been the work of God. He has reconciled us men to himself through Christ, and he has enlisted us in this service of reconciliation."

12. Romans 10:11-13 (NEB): "Scripture says, 'Everyone who has faith in him will be saved from shame'— everyone: there is no distinction between Jew and Greek, because the same Lord is Lord of all, and is rich enough for the need of all who invoke him. 'For everyone,' as it says again—'everyone who invokes the name of the Lord will be saved.'"

13. Romans 2:11, 14 (NEB): "For God has no favourites ... When Gentiles who do not possess the law carry out its precepts by the light of nature, then, although they have no law, they are their own law."

"And Scripture, foresee-ing that God would jus-tify the Gentiles through faith, declared the Gos-pel to Abraham before-hand: 'In you all nations shall find blessing.' Thus it is the men of faith who share the blessing with faithful Abraham."

15. *Genesis 1:29 (NEB): "God also said, 'I give you all plants that bear seed everywhere on earth, and every tree bearing fruit which yields seed; they shall be yours for food."*

16. *John 14:20 (NIV): "On that day you will realize that I am in my Father, and you are in me, and I am in you."*

17. *Galatians 2:20 (NIV): "I have been crucified with Christ and I no longer live, but Christ lives in me. The life I live in the body, I live by faith in the Son of God, who loved me and gave him-self for me."*

18. *Revelation 3:20 (NIV): "Here I am. I stand at the door and knock. If anyone hears my voice and opens the door, I will go in and eat with him, and he with me."*

19. *I Corinthians 6:19, 20 (NEB): "Do you not know that your body is a shrine of the indwelling Holy Spirit, and the Spirit is God's gift to you? You do not belong to yourselves; you were bought at a price. Then honour God in your body."*

20. *I Peter 2:5 (NEB): "Come, and let your-selves be built, as living stones, into a spiritual temple; become a holy priesthood, to offer spir-itual sacrifices accept-able to God through Jesus Christ."*

21. *Ephesians 2:22 (NEB): "In him you too are being built with all the rest into a spiritual dwelling for God."*

and is not always able to exert such control. Herein lies the most important component of the healthful lifestyle: a living trusting relationship with the God who created and redeemed his people (16 through 23).

When someone has that relationship, when he knows God so well that he can comfortably let Him live within, to manage and control his life, then there is also power to master the senses and to place them in proper perspective to the rest of life's needs. And with God living within, compliance to the laws that give health becomes not only possible and profitable, but often enjoyable as well.

These blessings were not given to the believers of the Adventist movement to be kept to themselves. They were to be shared with the world, to be a blessing to the world, and to serve as a tool to draw the world to its Savior. Indeed, when the love of the Master dwells within someone he cannot help but share with the hurting world around him—or so Adventists suggest.

To facilitate such sharing, extensive instruction was given regarding the means whereby they might share these blessings. Health care institutions, health food industries, medical missionary outreach programs, and services to the deprived peoples of the world have all been part of the message.

What has been its impact in the world? Only eternity will tell. But a few things are evident even now. The food industry is an interesting place to start. Were it not for such Adventist people as the Kellogg brothers, Harry Miller, and other physicians and food scientists searching for more economical and healthful ways to feed the world, the whole breakfast cereal industry would not exist. Peanut butter, soy milk (a lifesaver for untold millions of Oriental babies as well as for certain Western babies who have intolerances to milk), meat analogues, extenders, and substitutes, and a host of other items would be absent today from the food market.

Adventist health teams and acute care institutions circle the globe with quality health care. In these insti-tutions, hurting people find compassionate workers assisting nature's healing laws with the latest of mod-ern medical technology. For many, this professional touch of love serves as the means of introducing Chris-tianity to those who are unfamiliar with God's beauti-ful rescue plan for the world.

Adventists have been the focal point of study of many researchers attempting to find answers to the present epidemics of heart disease and cancer prevalent in Western society in the twentieth century. This is true because Adventists on the average live a number of years longer and experience less illness than the general population. For example, the death rate from coronary artery disease in the United States is taking a downward curve closely paralleling the institution of those measures for control that have been discovered in the study of Adventist lifestyle habits and which were initially revealed to Ellen White in vision.

From earliest times, the Advent believers have been active in educating people regarding the adverse effects of tobacco, alcohol, caffeine, and numerous other drugs. Temperance societies and publications have been strongly supported by Adventist believers through the years.

The facts that approximately fifty percent of all accidental deaths among adults involve alcohol and drugs, and that tobacco related illness accounts for by far the largest share of the health care dollar in the western world indicate that even though the warning has usually not been heard, the concerns regarding the devastating effects of intemperance are very valid. These facts are well accepted by present day scientists, but until very recently Adventist teachings regarding preventive medicine and healthful lifestyles were largely ignored and denied by the scientific and medical community.

Restaurants serving healthful food and teaching health principles to their customers: Health recovery programs where people suffering from the ravages of the modern lifestyle may spend a few weeks regaining their sense of direction and improving their health: Inner city ministries teaching the destitute and discouraged better survival means: All of these are other methods which the Advent believers have developed in order to reach the world with the saving grace of Jesus and to glorify His name.

What does all this say about Adventism as a cult? or as non-Christian? Just this: the whole message of Christianity is a message of a loving God reaching down to a race lost in sin and rebellion in an attempt to save them. It is a message of restoration. A careful look at the fruits of cults indicates that although they may have positive virtues, the overall effect is one of de-

22. II Corinthians 4:6 (NEB): "For the same God who said, 'Out of darkness let light shine,' has caused his light to shine within us, to give the light of revelation—the revelation of the glory of God in the face of Jesus Christ."

23. Isaiah 49:6 (NIV): "It is too slight a task for you, as my servant, to restore the tribes of Jacob, to bring back the descendants of Israel: I will make you a light to the nations, to be my salvation to earth's farthest bounds."

24. Matthew 7:20 (NIV): "Thus, by their fruit you will recognize them."

25. James 3:17 (NIV): "But the wisdom that comes from heaven is first of all pure; then peace loving, considerate, submissive, full of mercy and good fruit, impartial, and sincere."

struction and is contrary to the very purpose of the plan of God. "By their fruits ye shall know them" (24, 25). Does the health message of Adventism tend to build or destroy the cause of God among men? That is the question.

Adventists agree with other concerned Christians that legalistic obedience to the restrictions and regulations that Paul talked about in his epistles will not be a passport to heaven. They do not believe Paul is condemning in these statements obedience to sound laws that contribute to human health and happiness which in turn may aid and abet the cause of the Gospel. In view of this, Adventists deny any cultic connotations in the health doctrine.

Chapter IX

Dead or Alive?:
What Happens at the Time of Death?

"The serpent was more crafty than any wild creature that the Lord God had made. He said to the woman, 'Is it true that God has forbidden you to eat from any tree in the Garden?' (1) The woman answered the serpent, 'We may eat the fruit of any tree in the Garden except for the tree in the middle of the Garden; God has forbidden us either to eat or to touch the fruit of that; if we do, we will die.' The serpent said, 'OF COURSE YOU WILL NOT DIE' " (emphasis supplied) (Genesis 3:1-4, NEB).

Satan (speaking through the serpent) began his domination over man by convincing our first ancestors that God was withholding from them some very valuable information. Even more than that, he convinced Adam and Eve that God's statement to them that they would die if they partook of the fruit was a lie, and that instead of dying they would gain access to the knowledge that would make them like gods.

The devil's ploy was successful in accomplishing what he set out to do. The tool thus employed has remained one of his most effective instruments in leading people to a misconception of God and, hence, a rejection of His loving advances.

There is evidence very early in recorded history of a widespread belief that life continues after death. From the earliest days of Hinduism, Buddhism, and other ancient religions, there was nearly universal expectation of life beyond the grave—in one form or another. Death in the sense of cessation of existence was not even seriously considered. In ancient Babylon, in Egypt, and in Syria, the same teaching prevailed. It formed a very prominent position in later Greek and Roman philosophy as well.

The record coming down through the ancient Biblical patriarchs is a much different picture. The book of Genesis states that God created Adam from the earth and breathed into him the breath of life and he became a living soul (2). There is nothing in the text describing man's creation that suggests that God placed a soul within him that would later depart and return to God at the time of death, and there is nothing in the records

1. Genesis 2:16, 17 (NEB): "He told the man, 'You may eat from every tree in the garden, but not from the tree of the knowledge of good and evil; for on the day that you eat from it, you will certainly die.'"

2. Genesis 2:7 (NIV): "The Lord God formed the man from the dust of the ground and breathed into his nostrils the breath of life, and the man became a living being."

3. *Genesis 3:19 (NEB):* "You shall gain your bread by the sweat of your brow until you return to the ground; for from it you were taken. Dust you are, to dust you shall return."

4. *Psalms 115:17 (NEB):* "It is not the dead who praise the Lord, not those who go down into silence."

5. *Psalms 146:4 (NEB):* "He breathes his last breath, he returns to the dust; and in that same hour all his thinking ends."

6. *Ecclesiastes 9:5, 6 (NEB):* "True, the living know that they will die; but the dead know nothing. There are no more rewards for them; they are utterly forgotten. For them love, hate, ambition, all are now over. Never again will they have any part in what is done here under the sun."

7. *John 11:11 (NIV):* "After he had said this, he went on to tell them, 'Our friend Lazarus has fallen asleep; but I am going there to wake him up.'"

8. *Mark 5:39 (NIV):* "He went in and said to them, 'Why all this commotion and wailing? The child is not dead but asleep.'"

9. *Daniel 12:2 (NIV):* "Multitudes who sleep in the dust of the earth will awake: some to everlasting life, others to shame and everlasting contempt.'"

10. *Acts 13:36 (NIV):* "For when David had served God's purpose in his own generation, he fell asleep; he was buried with his fathers and his body decayed."

11. *I Thessalonians 4:14, 16 (NEB):* "We believe that Jesus died and rose again; and so it will be for those who died as Christians; God will bring them to life with Jesus ... because at the word of command, at the sound of the archangel's voice and God's trumpet-call, the Lord himself will descend from heaven; first the Christian dead will rise ... "

of man's fall that suggests that the devil's lie was true (3). Over and over again in scripture the concept is expressed that there is no consciousness, no thought in the grave to which men all must go. The Jews as a people clung to these ancient beliefs until Roman times (4 through 6.)

While the major thrust of the Holy Scriptures clearly teaches that the first death, that which all experience, is in reality nothing more than a sleep awaiting the resurrection (7 through 11), it must be admitted that there are a few passages that could be interpreted otherwise if taken by themselves and without a careful study of the context (Matthew 10:28; II Corinthians 5:1-10; Luke 16:19-21). A careful examination of these texts, however, allows them to fit easily into the overall theme supporting the position Adventists have taken—that God created human beings originally with the potential to live forever; that the entrance of sin into the world changed all that and brought death; but the gift of God through Jesus Christ will recover all who will accept recovery and they shall then live eternally (12-16).

Scripture is also very clear that there will be resurrections, a resurrection for the just when all who have accepted the redemption gift will arise to new life in a world renewed in its pristine glory (17, 18), and a resurrection for the wicked at which time the issues of the controversy between good and evil will be made clear and their destiny justified (19, 20). Adventists find it difficult to understand the purpose of a resurrection if a person is really not dead.

Many honest Christians wonder whether it makes a difference what one believes about the condition of the dead. Is a particular doctrine such as this going to effect my salvation already purchased by grace?

WHAT DIFFERENCE DOES IT MAKE WHAT ONE BELIEVES? JUST THIS—DOCTRINES OR BELIEFS HAVE NO MERIT IN AND OF THEMSELVES. THEIR MERIT OR DEMERIT RESIDES IN THE EFFECT THEY PRODUCE IN THE BELIEVER.

For example, Adventists believe that an incorrect understanding of the state of the dead opens the way for two critically damaging effects to occur that may interfere with one's salvation. If one accepts Satan's lie that men do not die, one is placed in the position of uncertainty as to how to deal with paraphysical phenomena and the whole world of spiritualism and the occult.

To believe that the dead are alive and that they may have access to information that the living do not, is to open the person up to a whole gamut of potential deceptions that "these souls" may introduce, for who is to say that they cannot communicate with the living? Adventists believe that the whole world of the occult represents Satan and his forces of evil actively engaged in battle against God and His people rather than the souls of the dead as so often claimed (21, 22).

In Old Testament times the Israelites were instructed to eradicate anyone and everyone who dealt with the occult (23, 24). The Apostle Paul in the New Testament, writing in various of his letters, identifies Satan as the active agent in occult experience (Acts 13:6-10) (25). He describes the war that Satan is waging and admonishes human beings to be wary and to put on the whole armor of God in their battle with evil (Ephesians 6:11). Adventits believe that Satan's final struggle will involve the utilization of this false doctrine in his attempt to deceive the world and win the battle away from God (Revelation 13:14).

The other major damaging effect has to do with the picture that may be painted of God when the belief is prevalent that God takes satisfaction and pleasure in punishing the wicked eternally. There are earnest Christians who believe that the doctrine of eternal punishment actually glorifies God by demonstrating His justice. Adventists do not accept such Biblical interpretation.

The Adventist position as they believe is taught in Holy Scripture is that God is indeed just and that sinners will reap the harvest of their lives, but that it will be in the most compassionate and loving way possible (26-29). They believe that the Scriptural warning of punishment was intended to mean that destruction that will be final, complete, and eternal; rather than the more commonly taught concept of fire that never ends (30 through 32). (For further consideration, study the following Bible examples: Genesis 19:1-29 and Jude 7; Isaiah 34:5, 8-11.) God's act of final annihilation of the wicked is indeed a "strange act" that will undoubtedly cause God great sorrow (33). This sadness can only be overshadowed by the joy and satisfaction of knowing that such an experience of sin will never happen again in His universe.

12. Ezekiel 18:4 (NIV): "For every living soul belongs to me, the father as well as the son—both alike belong to me. The soul who sins is the one who will die."

13. Romans 6:23 (NIV): "For the wages of sin is death, but the gift of God is eternal life in Christ Jesus our Lord."

14. John 3:15 (KJV): "That whosoever believeth in him should not perish, but have eternal life."

15. I Corinthians 15:52, 53 (NEB): "For the trumpet will sound, and the dead will rise immortal, and we shall be changed. This perishable being must be clothed with the imperishable, and what is mortal must be clothed with immortality."

16. Revelation 18:20 (NEB): "But let heaven exult over her; exult, apostles and prophets and people of God; for in the judgment against her he has vindicated your cause!"

17. Hebrews 11:13-16 (NEB): "All these persons died in faith. They were not yet in possession of the things promised, but had seen them far ahead and hailed them, and confessed themselves no more than strangers or passing travellers on earth. Those who use such language show plainly that they are looking for a country of their own. If their hearts had been in the country they had left, they could have found opportunity to return. Instead, we find them longing for a better country—I mean, the heavenly one. That is why God is not ashamed to be called their God; for he has a city ready for them."

18. I Thessalonians 4:14, 16, 17 (NEB): "We believe that Jesus died and rose again; and so it will be for those who died as Christians; God will bring them to life with Jesus ... because at the word of command, at the sound of the archangel's voice and God's trumpet-call, the Lord himself will descend from heaven; first the Christian dead will rise, then we who are left alive shall join them, caught up in clouds to meet the Lord in the air."

19. Revelation 20:5 (NEB): "... though the rest of the dead did not come to life until the thousand years were over. This was the first resurrection."

20. John 5:28, 29 (NEB): "Do not wonder at this, because the time is coming when all who are in the grave shall hear his voice and come out:those who have done right will rise to life; those who have done wrong will rise to hear their doom."

21. Ephesians 6:12 (NEB): "For our fight is not against human foes, but against cosmic powers, against the authorities and potentates of this dark world, against the super human forces of evil in the heavens."

22. Revelation 12:9, 12 (NEB): "So the great dragon was thrown down, that serpent of old that led the whole world astray, whose name is Satan, or the Devil—thrown down to the earth, and his angels with him ... 'Rejoice then, you heavens and you that dwell in them! But woe to you, earth and sea, for the Devil has come down to you in great fury, knowing that his time is short!'"

23. Leviticus 20:6 (NEB): "I will set my face against the man who wantonly resorts to ghosts and spirits, and I will cut that person off from his people."

24. Leviticus 19:26, 28 (NEB): "You shall not eat meat with the blood in it. You shall not practice divination or soothsaying ... You shall not gash yourselves in mourning for the dead; you shall not tattoo yourselves. I am the Lord."

To see that this is an accurate portrayal of the loving character of God, one need only to look at the way Jesus dealt with sin while He lived on earth. Look at the example of Mary when caught in the act of adultery (John 7:53-8:11). Note again His patience and Mary's accusers. (He revealed their secret sins, but only to themselves) (34). Note again His patience and kindness to Mary (35). Adventists believe that they have ample evidence throughout Scriptures to indicate the kind of God they serve. They believe that one of the most successful campaigns that Satan has waged against God has been this one of painting God as a God of vengeance and revenge.

They concede that the Bible speaks often of the wrath of God and God's anger. But the Bible is also clear that God's wrath is an act of love; like that of a father who must deal with a precious but rebellious son (36 through 38). In all instances, his wrath is that which happens to individuals when they separate themselves from His love and place themselves where He can no longer touch them with healing (39, 40). Always, it is used to discipline and correct His people and only becomes destructive when they have separated far beyond any possibility of reconciliation. And even then it is an act of love (Thompson, 1988, 48-58).

Adventists believe that no doctrine has done more to distort the true nature of God's love than the doctrine of the eternal torment of the wicked based upon the concept of an immortal soul. Through the centuries untold millions have rejected God and His whole plan of salvation because it is impossible for them to accept that such punishment is consistent with true love. The devil did his homework well! It is sometimes difficult for new converts to the faith to forsake the lifelong belief that their loved ones go immediately to heaven or hell when they die, but rather return to the dust from which they were created (41). When, however, the full impact of the beauty of God's total plan of restoration is understood and it is realized that their loved ones who have died are not really being tormented in hell, or in need of purchase from purgatory, or even in heaven looking down upon our troubled lives, then they are able to rejoice in their new-found faith and their clearer, more complete picture of God's love and the blessed hope.

The doctrine regarding the state of the dead is not subject to scientific proof. It must be accepted by faith.

Adventists believe that the weight of Scriptural evidence is heavily on the side of man as a being composed of a body into which God has placed His breath of life to become a living soul. On resurrection morning, Adventists believe God's followers will be resurrected, again in God's image, but this time immortal, never to die again (for sin will not interfere a second time).

Does such faith merit the Seventh-day Adventist church the label of a cult? Each reader must answer this question for himself, but Adventists would contend that the Holy Bible is their best defense.

The next chapter will discuss Adventist teachings regarding end-time events. Throughout that discussion, one should note how knowledge regarding the state of the dead might play a role in Satan's deceptions in his last bid to defeat his foe. Adventists believe this is an important concept to understand if people would avoid Satan's trap.

REFERENCES

Fudge, Edward W. The Fire that Consumes. Houston, TX: Providential Press, 1982.

Thompson, Walter C., M.D. Pearls and Pills. Amherst, WI: Palmer Publications, Inc., 1988.

25. Acts 13:8, 10 (NIV): "But Elymas the sorcerer (for that is what his name means) opposed them and tried to turn the proconsul from the faith . . . 'You are a child of the devil and an enemy of everything that is right! You are full of all kinds of deceit and trickery. Will you never stop perverting the right ways of the Lord?'"

26. Deuteronomy 32:4 (NEB): " . . . the creator whose work is perfect, and all his ways are just, a faithful god, who does no wrong, righteous and true is He!"

27. Genesis 18:25 (NIV): "Far be it from you to do such a thing—to kill the righteous with the wicked alike. Far be it from you! Will not the Judge of all the earth do right?"

28. Proverbs 11:3 (NIV): "The integrity of the upright guides them, but the unfaithful are destroyed by their duplicity."

29. Proverbs 11:21 (NIV): "Be sure of this: The wicked will not go unpunished, but those who are righteous will go free."

30. II Peter 3:7 (NEB): "And the present heavens and earth, again by God's word, have been kept in store for burning; they are being reserved until the day of judgment when the godless will be destroyed."

31. Nahum 1:8, 9 (NEB): " . . . and brings them safely through the sweeping flood; he makes a final end of all who oppose him and pursues his enemies into darkness. No adversaries dare oppose him twice; all are burnt up like tangled briars."

32. Romans 9:28 (NEB): " . . . for the Lord's sentence on the land will be summary and final . . ."

33. Isaiah 28:21 (NEB): "But the Lord shall arise as he rose on Mount Perazim and storm with rage as he did in the Vale of Gibeon to do what he must do—how strange a deed! to perform his work—how outlandish a work!"

34. John 8:7-9 (NIV): "When they kept on questioning him, he straightened up and said to them, 'If any one of you is without sin, let him be the first to throw a stone at her.' Again he stooped down and wrote on the ground. At this, those who heard began to go away one at a time, the older ones first, until only Jesus was left, with the woman still standing there."

35. John 8:10, 11 (NIV): " . . . Woman, where are they? Has no one condemned you? 'No one, sir,' she said.'"

36. Revelation 3:19 (NEB): "All whom I love I reprove and discipline. Be on your mettle therefore and repent."

37. Lamentations 3:22, 23, 32, 33 (NEB): "The Lord's true love is surely not spent, nor has his compassion failed; they are new every morning, so great is his constancy . . . He may punish cruelly, yet he will have compassion in the fullness of his love; he does not willingly afflict or punish any mortal man."

38. Hebrews 12:6, 10 (NEB): " . . . for the Lord disciplines those whom he loves; he lays the rod on every son whom he acknowledges . . . They disciplined us for this short life according to their lights; but he does so for our true welfare, so that we may share his holiness."

39. Romans 1:24, 25, 28 (NEB): "For this reason God has given them up to the vileness of their own desires, and the consequent degradation of their bodies, because they have bartered away the true God for a false one, and have offered reverence and worship to created things instead of to the Creator, who is blessed forever; amen . . . Thus, because they have not seen fit to acknowledge God, he has given them up to their own depraved reason."

40. Psalms 81:12 (NEB): " . . . so I sent them off, stubborn as they were, to follow their own devices."

41. Genesis 3:19 (NEB): " . . . for from it you were taken. Dust you are, to dust you shall return."

Chapter X

End-Time Events

"After this I saw another angel coming down from heaven; he came with great authority and the earth was lit up with his splendour. Then a mighty voice proclaimed, 'fallen, fallen is Babylon the great . . .' Then I heard another voice from heaven that said, 'Come out of her, my people, lest you take part in her sins and share in her plagues' " (Revelation 18:1-4, NEB).

Seventh-day Adventists believe that the prophecies of the Bible are true and that they are understandable to the people and the times to which they apply. They believe that these are the last days of this world's history and that the Bible prophecies concerning the "last days" apply to this generation. If this is true, they reason, then these same Bible prophecies ought reasonably be understood by those honestly seeking truth (1, 2). Adventists believe that, as already discussed elsewhere, the Advent Movement was designed and instituted by God to call the peoples of the world from sin and to God in sincerity and honesty, for the end of all things is at hand. They envision their sole purpose for existance to be that of warning and invitation: warning regarding the impending consequence of sin, and invitation to join in the family of God and to share in the blessings of the kingdom.

Because of this conviction and because of Adventist teachings regarding their role in these end-time events, Seventh-day Adventism is sometimes viewed by others as appearing to be elite, oppositional, too good for the society of others, separate, etc.—all marks of a cult. Is the concern warranted?

Adventists believe that when Jesus returns there will be just two groups of people living on earth: those who have accepted His saving Grace, and those who have rejected it (3). There will be those who are identified with His seal (4), and those bearing the mark of the enemy (5). The former group epitomizes truth and goodness, for they have allowed the Spirit of God to dwell within and to write His law upon their hearts and minds. The other group epitomizes selfishness and deception, for they have yielded themselves to the power of Satan by choice or by default. As the controv-

1. Jeremiah 29:13 (NIV): "You will seek me and find me when you seek me with all your heart."

2. John 8:32 (NIV): "Then you will know the truth, and the truth will set you free."

3. Matthew 25:31, 32 (NIV): "When the Son of Man comes in his glory, and all the angels with him, he will sit on his throne in heavenly glory. All the nations will be gathered before him, and he will separate the people one from another as a shepherd separates the sheep from the goats."

4. Revelation 7:2, 3 and 14:1 (NIV): "Then I saw another angel coming from the east, having been given power to harm the land and the sea: 'Do not harm the land or the sea or the trees until we put a seal on the foreheads of the servants of out Gos.' . . . Who had His name and His Father's name written on their foreheads."

5. Revelation 13:16 (NIV): "He also forced everyone, small and great, rich and poor, free and slave, to receive a mark on his right hand or on his forehead."

ersy between good and evil enters its final battle (Armageddon), these two will meet in life and death conflict. As time runs out for the human race and the last pleas for mercy are accepted or rejected, the true character of both good and evil will be clearly demonstrated. Then it will be seen by all living intelligent beings exactly how the nature of True Love contrasts with the malignancy of sin.

6. Revelation 18:2-4 (NIV): "With a mighty voice he shouted: 'Fall! Fallen is Babylon the Great! She has become a home for demons and a haunt for every evil spirit, a haunt for every unclean and detestable bird. For all the nations have drunk the maddening wine of her adulteries. The kings of the earth committed adultery with her, and the merchants of the earth grew rich from her excessive luxuries.' Then I heard another voice from heaven say: 'Come out of her, my people, so that you will not share in her sins, so that you will not receive any of her plagues.'"

The Bible speaks prophetically of the fall of Babylon (the symbol of confusion and worldliness under the direction of Satan) and of the ultimate victory of the saints of God and the New Jerusalem (6).

In heaven, before he was cast out, Satan declared the principles of his rebellion. "I will be like the most High, I will . . . I will . . . .I will . . ." (Isaiah 14:12-14). We see in this passage a focus upon self-glory and exaltation. It is as if the self-sacrificing love governing the kingdom of God is ineffective and inhibiting, precluding the development of the full potential of intelligent beings, undoubtedly held in check by a hypocritical God who only claims self-sacrificing love, expecting it of His creatures, but secretly protecting His own domain thereby.

We hear a similar insinuation in Eden as Satan wrestles with Eve. "Is it true that God has forbidden you to eat from any tree in the garden?" (Genesis 3:1). "God knows that as soon as you eat of it your eyes will be opened and you will be like gods . . ." (Genesis 3:5). The record shows that Adam and Eve lost their garden home and introduced rebellion into the human race because they accepted the principles of Satan's rebellion and partook of his same spirit. They, too, could be a god unto themselves and climb to whatever level of power they were willing to strive to attain.

Cain, the first son born into the human family, demonstrated that already back then the principle had affixed itself to human thought and action. The gift of produce that he offered to God upon his altar was the best he had to give, but it was the gift of his own devising, not an acknowledgment of the power and authority of his Creator (Genesis 4:1-16).

As one notes Biblical and secular history since that time, one sees throughout the exaltation of the self and the expression of one's own desires, wisdom, and opinions rather than faithful submission to the claims and instructions of God. Such is the nature of Satan's kingdom, such are the principles of Babylon the capital of his domain. Though the Biblical record before the flood describes this principle in action, it is important to look to the record following the flood to find the roots for the present age. The Bible describes this rebellion in its story about the Tower of Babel. In this story, human beings ignore God's promises given in the symbol of the rainbow and begin to build a tower that will reach above the deepest flood waters, "just in case" (Genesis 11:1-9).

Secular history records similar stories, but also tells of the beginnings of religious philosophies and practices centering around worship to the gods of the sun and moon and other created works. Indeed, of all the ancient cultures on the seven continents, one sees religion focused upon salvation by one's own works, often gained by pleasing the gods shaped like created things. Ancient Israel at first struggled with these gods but eventually adopted most of them and honored them side by side with their creator God.

Soon after Jesus came to show the world the fallacy of idolatry and to unfold the goodness of His kingdom of grace, the principles of Satan's dominion began to creep into the Christian church (II Thessalonians 2:3-8). Forms of worship, religious symbols, philosophies and attitudes derived directly from neighboring pagan religions infiltrated the Christian worship services. Icons, statues and monuments were moved to Christian churches from the ancient pagan shrines and Christian names were given to pagan gods. Burdened by such a handicap, the Christian church struggled through those early centuries. It nearly collapsed during the long Dark Ages of Papal dominance, saved only by small companies of God's faithful in various places on earth.

With the Protestant Reformation, hope again sprang up. People searched the Scriptures to learn the will and purpose of God. Unfortunately, though great truths were unearthed and strong Christian reformers experienced freedom in Christ, a decline of godliness rapidly resulted with the death of the reformers. Again, Satan subtly introduced his errors into the reformed churches. False doctrines distorting the love and goodness of God, and as ancient as Babylon itself, tethered the work of God among men and hindered the work He must accomplish before His return.

But Satan never gained the allegiance of the whole race. Throughout history God has had His faithful followers, too—from the early days until now. To find them will not be too difficult, for the Bible has already listed many of them in order during the first four thousand years. They are listed in the Book of Hebrews, Chapter 11.

Beginning with Abel (whom Cain killed), down through the ages, one reads of Enoch, Noah, Abraham, and Sarah. Note the characteristics: "Anyone who comes to God must believe that He exists" (Hebrews 11:6, NEB). "By faith, Noah, divinely warned about the unseen future, took heed and built an ark to save his household. Through faith he put the whole world in the wrong, and made good his own claim to the righteousness that comes of faith" (verse 7). "By faith Abraham obeyed" (verse 8). "He settled in an alien land promised him" (verse 9). "For he was looking forward to the city with firm foundations whose architect and builder is God" (verse 10). All these persons died in faith. They were not yet in possession of the things promised, but had seen them far ahead and hailed them and confessed themselves no more than strangers or passing travelers on earth. We find them longing for a better country—a heavenly one. That is why God is not ashamed to be called their God (verses 13, 16). "For he [Abraham] reckoned that God had power even to raise from the dead" (verse 19). "By faith Moses, when he grew up, refused to be called the son of Pharoah's daughter, preferring to suffer hardship with the people of God rather than enjoy the transient pleasures of sin. He considered the stigma that rests on God's annointed greater wealth than the treasures of Egypt" (verse 24-26). "By faith he left Egypt, and not because he was fearful of the king's anger; for he was resolute, as one who saw the invisible God" (verse 27). "By faith the prostitute Rehab escaped the doom of unbelievers" (verse 31). "Stories of Gideon, Barak, Samson, and Jephthah, of David and Samuel and the prophets. Through faith they overthrew kingdoms, established justice, saw God's promises fulfilled" (verse 32, 33). "Others were tortured to death, disdaining release, to win a better resurrection. Others again had to face flogging, even fetters and prison bars. They were stoned, they were sawn in two, they were put to the sword, they went dressed in skin of sheep and goats, in poverty, distress, and misery. THEY WERE TOO GOOD FOR A WORLD LIKE THIS. They were refugees in deserts and on the hills,

74

hiding in caves and holes in the ground. These also, one and all, are commemorated for their faith" (emphasis supplied) (verses 35-39).

It has been no different in the Christian era. The records are clear—those who by faith have been obedient to the cause of truth have often defended it with their life. Millions of faithful have suffered and died through the centuries at the hands of the Christian church. Always there have been those who have believed the truth about God (as recorded in the Bible), a belief that caused them to sacrifice everything if need be for the cause they believed in. Adventists believe this has always been the true mark of God's followers and will be until the end (7, 8).

Having pictured two groups of people, those living according to the principles of Babylon, the world of Satan, and those following the principles of self-sacrificing love through faith, as exemplified in Jesus, it is time to examine what the Adventist interpretation says about the struggle.

For the past few centuries in most parts of the world, God's people have blended well with the peoples of the world. It has been a period of relative religious tolerance (there have been some major exceptions). The work of the Gospel has gone forward to the ends of the earth with relatively little opposition. A world has been preparing for the final events and the return of the Lord.

Recently, as the world struggles with moral decline, economic instability, population explosion and mass starvation, reality of nuclear catastrophy, environmental pollution, loss of natural resources, and a thousand and one other concerns, one may note that the religious world—though fragmented for centuries—is beginning to rally together in an effort to find resolution to the things that threaten the continued existence of planet Earth.

This is as anticipated, for the Holy Bible predicts just such struggles at the end of time (9). Adventists have long believed and taught that events just such as these would be the catalysts that would trigger the final scenes of earth history (White, 590-591). As the world begins to reap the harvest of the seed that it has sown, the peoples of the earth recognize that they must unite if they would change the otherwise inevitable course. Unfortunately, the means chosen to solve the problems are not the means by which the Creator

7. John 15:20 (NIV): "Remember the words I spoke to you: 'No servant is greater than his master.' If they persecuted me, they will persecute you also.'"

8. II Timothy 3:12 (NIV): "In fact, everyone who wants to live a godly life in Christ Jesus will be persecuted."

9. Revelation 12:17 through 13:17 (NIV): "Then the dragon was enraged at the woman and went off to make war against the rest of her offspring—those who obey God's commandments and hold to the testimony of Jesus. And the dragon stood on the shore of the sea. And I saw a beast coming out of the sea. He had ten horns and seven heads, with ten crowns on his horns, and on each head a blasphemous name. The beast I saw resembled a leopard but had feet like those of a bear and a mouth like that of a lion. The dragon gave the beast his power and his throne and great authority. One of the heads of the beast seemed to have had a fatal wound, but the fatal wound had been healed. The whole world was astonished and followed the beast. Men worshipped the dragon because he had given authority to the beast, and they also worshipped the beast and asked, 'Who is like the beast? Who can make war against him?' The beast was given a mouth to utter proud words and blasphemies and to exercise his authority for forty-two months. He opened his mouth to blaspheme God and to slander his name and his dwelling place and those who live in heaven. He was given power to make war against the saints and to conquer them. And he was given authority over every tribe, people, language, and nation. All inhabitants whose names have not been written in the book of life belonging to the lamb that was slain from the creation of the world. He who has an ear, let him hear. If anyone is to go into captivity, into captivity he will go. If anyone is to be killed with the sword, with the

10. *Luke 13:3 (NIV): "I tell you, no! But unless you repent, you too will all perish."*

11. *John 4:24 (NIV): "God is spirit, and his worshippers must worship in spirit and in truth."*

admonished His children (10, 11). Instead of honestly repenting of evil and meeting the crises by applying the principles of His kingdom, human wisdom seeks its solution through the only means with which it is familiar, by applying the principles of Babylon; i.e., bribes or force. Accordingly, Adventists believe that the prophecies of Revelation found in Chapters 13 to 18 describe with symbols the tensions and the outcome of the conflict that will occur at the end-time, and indeed have already begun.

According to Adventist interpretation, the lamb-like beast with two horns described in Revelation, Chapter 13, refers to the United States (Revelation 13:11). This nation, developing closely on the heals of the reformation, was founded upon true Christian principles. Freedom of the individual to worship his God according to conscience was a major tenant. Church and state were designed to function separately to the benefit of both.

As a consequence, many Adventists believe, it has enjoyed more than two hundred years of prosperity and relative peace. It has been the home base from which missionaries carrying the gospel have gone out into the whole world. It has facilitated the promulgation of Christian principles around the circle of the earth.

But the prophecy predicts a change in the character of this "gentle" beast. "He had two horns like a lamb, but he spoke like a dragon" (Revelation 13:11). No longer sporting freedom, it begins to make laws and enforce them with threats and death decrees. Whereas the nation was established in a way to clearly separate government from religion, the change that occurs happens as religion unites its power and authority with the state. Bonded together in common cause to solve the problems threatening extinction, legislation is written, courts are convened, and executive power is mobilized. Working together, they believe that dissident citizens and conscience-bound "fanatics" (the major cause of the universal troubles affecting the land) can be brought to compliance, by force if need be.

The reader might well ask, what kind of behavior could elicit such a response by the state (Revelation 13:15)? What kind of activity is such a threat to society that a decree of death is warranted, as suggested in the Scripture?

Certainly it will not be aimed at lying, for lying and

deception have come to make up the very warp and woof of business and economic society. Likewise, stealing—man cheats and steals as easily as he winks his eyes. Adultery and sexual immorality just might create a stir, but who in their land could cast the first stone? Nearly all have rationalized away the command and made it of no effect, in thought if not in deed. Even murder, though still kept fairly well controlled by civil force, is not foreign to angry thoughts, nor is anyone apt to condemn one for coveting his neighbor's car or house, so long as he leaves it alone. So it seems obvious that the crime that the Bible talks about as necessitating a death decree must not have to do with civil disobedience in interpersonal affairs. If not, what?

The Scripture states that it will be those who refuse to worship the beast and receive its mark in the forehead and in the hand that will be so severely discriminated against (Revelation 13:15, 16). Adventists believe that the image of the beast referred to is the establishment of Sunday (an institution established upon the authority of the Roman Church) (11a) as a national holiday, legislated by the demand of protestant America. They believe that the mark refers to the obedience of that law which is opposed to the Sabbath of God described in the Bible.

11a. "Q. Which day is the Sabbath day?"
"A. Saturday is the Sabbath day."
"Q. Why do we observe Sunday instead of Saturday?"
"A. We observe Sunday instead of Saturday because the Catholic Church transferred the solemnity from Saturday to Sunday." (Geiermann, 1977, 50)

Since Adventists believe that the Sabbath commandment is God's mark or seal of authority (refer to chapter regarding Sabbath) they will find themselves in conflict with the laws of the land when legislation is passed requiring observation of Sunday sacredness.

It might seem strange that Adventists would build their interpretation of prophetic Scripture around such an apparently insignificant thing as a particular day upon which to worship God. Why, if their claim that eternal destiny is determined by belief or unbelief in God; and true fellowship in the family of God depends upon a righteous life of obedience made possible through grace, by faith, do they place so much emphasis upon the Sabbath?

The answer must be found again in the setting of worship and the principles of the two rival kingdoms, that of God and that of the archenemy. As the day of the sun has been a symbol of allegiance to the principles of Satan since the days of ancient Babylon, and as it has been identified as the mark of the authority of the mother church by its own claim in more recent times, so the seventh-day Sabbath has symbolized allegiance to the God of creation and the principles of His kingdom from ancient times. Viewed from this perspective, the day is not the determining factor. Mere Sabbath observance has no merit toward achieving heaven, nor will Sunday worship prevent a true child of God from entering the pearly gates. But, when in time the day of worship becomes the legal and completely recognizable distinguishing sign, then to ignore God's sign is paramount to flaunting the banner of Satan.

In this sense, then, though the mark of the beast in the forehead and in the hand represents the mindset and actions of worldliness, and the seal of God represents belief in the principles of God's kingdom, there is a sense in which Sunday observance represents the mark of the beast (Adventists believe not until people have had opportunity to know and understand the difference can they be held accountable for Sunday observance) and Sabbath celebration the seal of God. Such statements as these may sound arrogant and even foolishly self-righteous to the non-Adventist Christian. After all, isn't it rather rash to identify all of the world's great religions as Babylon and to single Adventism out as the only followers of God? The question is a valid one. The Adventist answer would most often go something like this: "God is no respecter of persons. He cares nothing for labels that people place upon themselves or upon one another. He had only one purpose, to rescue a race fallen into sin and now at a point ready to self-destruct. Throughout the centuries He has had His chosen instruments who would by faith support His cause and consent to be His representatives. Sometimes these voices have been individuals or small groups of people, at other times large communities of believers or even whole nations. The Christian era has been no exception. The early Christian church was filled with zeal and by the power of the Spirit carried the Gospel to the whole known world. But the devil is active and determined. Little by little he worked his principles into the church of God until he had successufully undermined nearly the whole system. As the forces of the evil one gained increasing control, God was left more and more "holding the bag," as it were, as people joined the opposing army. Again and again God has raised up His messengers to fight for Him and defend His cause, and again and again they have been destroyed, driven underground, or have yielded to the enemy under heavy duress. But in spite of this God has always had a line of faithful followers who have remained loyal and true to Him and His cause.

In these times it is no different. Adventists believe that they have been raised up for a special purpose with a special message to bear. But, if there is a special message, there must be people to be reached. Adventists believe and teach that there are many of all faiths, Christian and non-Christian alike, who are following God to the best of their knowledge and understanding, and who love the Lord and their fellow man as dearly as any Adventist might hope to love (12). These, Adventists believe, must hear the invitation to come out of Babylon and partake not of her sins (13). Not only so, but Adventist teaching has long declared that coincident to the influx of the faithful into the family of God, many bearing the name of Adventist, but devoid of the indwelling Spirit of Christ, would be shaken out—even some of the brightest lights and most talented leaders (Hebrews 12:26-28). From this it is clear, at least in traditional Adventist thought, that the remnant who are finally ready to meet their Lord at His coming will be those of all faiths who have joined hands in the fellowship of obedience produced by love through faith. There is no Adventist sentiment against Catholics, Jews, Protestants, Hindus, Moslems, Buddhists, or any other persuasion. Only there is a recognition and proclamation that there are systems of religion that have become corrupted by sin that are not only destroying the cause of God in the world, but also the world itself that was given to be their home.

As this last generation experiences in increasing fury the harvest of sin, their frustration and anger will find expression upon the faithful of God. These in turn, aroused from their lukewarm state to the reality of their cause, will yield to the power of the Holy Spirit poured out in Pentacostal measure. Then will be fulfilled the prophecy that states, "The whole world will be filled with the glory of God" (14). Then it is that the faithful of all persuasions separate from Babylon and swell the numbers of the faithful. Identified with the seal of the living God (the characteristics of God implanted in their hearts) they will stand out in contrast to those bearing the mark of the beast. The Bible speaks of this time as the time of Jacob's trouble, and

12. Romans 2:11, 14, 15 (NEB): "For God does not show favoritism . . . Indeed, when Gentiles, who do not have the law, do by nature things required by the law, they are a law for themselves, even though they do not have the law, since they show that the requirements of the law are written on their hearts, their consciences also bearing witness, and their thoughts now accusing, now even defending them."

13. Revelation 18:4 (NIV): "Then I heard another voice from heaven say: 'Come out of her, my people, so that you will not share in her sins, so that you will not receive any of her plagues.'"

14. Revelation 18:1 (NIV): "After this I saw another angel coming down from heaven. He had great authority, and the earth was illuminated by his splendor."

79

15. Jeremiah 30:7 (NIV): "How awful that day will be! None will be like it. It will be a time of trouble for Jacob, but he will be saved out of it."

16. Revelation 15:1 (NIV): "I saw in heaven another great and marvelous sign: seven angels with the seven last plagues—last, because with them God's wrath is completed."

17. Hebrews 6:18 (NIV): "God did this so that by two unchangeable things in which it is impossible for God to lie, we who have fled to take hold of the hope offered to us may be greatly encouraged."

18. Ezekiel 33:11 (NIV): "Say to them, 'As surely as I live, declares the Sovereign Lord, I take no pleasure in the death of the wicked, but rather that they turn from their evil ways and live. Turn! Turn from your evil ways! Why will you die, O house of Israel?'"

describes it in most solemn terms (15). But the promises of Scripture support and maintain the faithful through the cruel, dark night until Jesus shall blow the trumpet in announcement of His coming.

While prophecy speaks of a time of trouble for the faithful, it also describes trouble for the unrepentant peoples of the world. As the plagues that fell upon Egypt in the days of Moses, disaster will again come upon the earth. As God finally, though reluctantly, withdraws His controlling hand and allows the full consequence of sin to work its malignant harvest, the earth will suffer such calamity as is impossible to describe (16).

This picture of end-times just painted is not a pretty picture for the men and women of the world, captured and held by the deceptive allusions of wealth, beauty, and power offered in symbolic Babylon. Adventists themselves tremble as they consider the magnitude of its implications. But the prophecies of the Bible cannot be wrong (17). And if not wrong, the place for Adventism is well defined.

Perhaps no one ought to be faulted for toying with the temptation to cinch their assignment of Adventism to the status of cult in view of the things herein revealed. Certainly, this study has touched upon a number of sensitive and in some ways incriminating issues. Yet, it is hoped, the reader will sense throughout the sentiment of a loving God reaching down through a submissive people to rescue a hurting and dying world. For the Adventist people, like God Himself, are "not willing for any to perish," (18) but desire that all turn from the intoxicating attractions of Babylon and be saved.

REFERENCE

White, Ellen G. The Great Controversy Between Christ and Satan. Mountain View, CA: Pacific Press Publishing Association, 1950.

Chapter XI

With Liberty and Justice for All: Separation of Church and State

Perhaps because of their beliefs regarding the final movements of earth's history, Adventists have taken an active role in supporting and promoting religious liberty. As noted elsewhere, they anticipate a time when this nation which was founded on the principles of representative government and the freedom of individual worship will legislate religious practice. This legislation they believe will focus on Sunday sacredness.

They believe the prophecy of Revelation 13 specifically referes to this nation and to these times. As a consequence, they have accepted as part of their charge the responsibility of maintaining that freedom upon which this nation was established. They accept this charge not because they believe that it will prevent or even delay the fulfillment of prophecy (although they would rejoice if the whole world were to follow the example of Nineveh and repent of its evil [Jonah, chapter 3]), but because they believe that the principles laid down in its constitution are God-given and representative of the freedom which God Himself has established in governing all of His creation (1, 2).

It was freedom of the individual to choose that allowed sin and rebellion to enter the universe and this earth. It was for the sake of that freedom that God paid the ultimate price. Although the sin experience has been a traumatic one for God and His creation, when it is completed, His universe will remain free forever (3, 4).

To defend this principle, Adventists lift their voices for the sake of men of all creeds. If in the process the attention of men is brought to focus upon the principles of God's love and they are forced to examine these principles in greater detail, it can only be to His glory.

The history of the Christian church has often been bloody; shame and contempt have been poured upon the name of Christ through persecution and martyrdom. Through the centuries millions of devout but non-conforming Christians have lost their lives to others professing the name of Christ whom, Advent-

1. *Joshua 24:15 (NIV): "But if serving the Lord seems undesirable to you, then choose for yourselves this day whom you will serve, whether the gods your forefathers served beyond the River, or the gods of the Amorites, in whose land you are living. But as for me and my household, we will serve the Lord."*

2. *Deuteronomy 30:19 (NIV): "This day I call heaven and earth as witnesses against you that I have set before you life and death, blessings and curses. Now choose life, so that you and your children may live . . ."*

3. *Romans 5:10 (NIV): "For if, when we were God's enemies, we were reconciled to him through the death of his Son, how much more, having been reconciled, shall we be saved through his life!"*

4. *Romans 8:2, 15, 21 (NIV): ". . . because through Christ Jesus the law of the Spirit of life set me free from the law of sin and death . . . For you did not receive a spirit that makes you a slave again to fear, but you received the Spirit of sonship. And by him we cry, 'Abba, Father . . .' that the creation itself will be liberated from its bondage to decay and brought into the glorious freedom of the children of God."*

5. *Romans 13:1-6 (NIV):* "*Everyone must submit himself to the governing authorities, for there is no authority except that which God has established. The authorities that exist have been established by God. Consequently, he who rebels against the authority is rebelling against what God has instituted, and those who do so will bring judgment on themselves. For rulers hold no terror for those who do right, but for those who do wrong. Do you want to be free from fear of the one in authority? Then do what is right and he will commend you. For he is God's servant to do you good. But if you do wrong, be afraid, for he does not bear the sword for nothing. He is God's servant, an agent of wrath to bring punishment on the wrongdoer. Therefore, it is necessary to submit to the authorities, not only because of possible punishment but also because of conscience. This is also why you pay taxes, for the authorities are God's servants, who give their full time to governing.*"

6. *I Peter 2:13-18 (NIV):* "*Submit yourselves for the Lord's sake to every authority instituted among men; whether to the king, as the supreme authority, or to governors, who are sent by him to punish those who do wrong and to commend those who do right. For it is God's will that by doing good you should silence the ignorant talk of foolish men. Live as free men, but do not use your freedom as a cover-up for evil; live as servants of God. Show proper respect to everyone: Love the brotherhood of believers, fear God, honor the king. Slaves, submit yourselves to your masters with all respect, not only to those who are good and considerate, but also to those who are harsh.*"

7. *Acts 5:29 (NIV):* "*Peter and the other apostles replied: 'We must obey God rather than men!'*"

8. *Acts 4:19 (NIV):* "*But Peter and John replied, 'Judge for yourselves whether it is right in God's sight to obey you rather than God. For we cannot help speaking what we have seen and heard.'*"

ists believe, were ignorant of the very principles of freedom expressed in His Gospel.

IF ANY CLEAR STATEMENT CAN BE MADE DIFFERENTIATING FALSE FROM TRUE RELIGION, IT MAY BE THIS: FALSE RELIGION IS WILLING TO KILL TO PROMOTE ITS CAUSE, WHEREAS TRUE RELIGION IS WILLING TO DIE THAT OTHERS MIGHT LIVE.

Adventists believe that government exists by the authority of God (5, 6). Its leaders are God's agents. Obedience is the obligation of all of its citizens. Only when governmental regulation and the word of God come into direct conflict, does governmental authority yield to the individual's obligation to God (7, 8). Adventists recognize that situations arise wherein the freedom of an individual may need to be sacrificed for the benefit of society as a whole (such as imprisonment or death for criminal behavior), but they also believe that it is the responsibility of government to defend the rights and freedoms of all of its citizens so long as that freedom does not interfere with the right and freedom of another.

While most Christians as well as many non-Christians acknowledge in word the concept of individual rights in matters of conscience, Adventists anticipate a time when the people of this land will, in the name of Christ, be willing to sacrifice these rights for the perceived good of society. In the mind of Adventists, such behavior is at variance with the picture of God that Scripture portrays and deserves exposure and warning.

For this interest in freedom of religion and the rights of all men, Adventists anticipate increasing resistance as man more closely approaches the end-time events. For this, should they be labeled a cult?

Chapter XII

Worship the Creator— Creation vs. Evolution: The Adventist Position

Small green shoots sprout out of the ground and burst into a thousand different hues. Lilies awakening from their long winter naps gently nudge their tender shoots through the cool dark earth. Tiny seeds each containing its own pre-programmed "chips" explode open and send little white shoots into the ground and green leaves toward heaven.

It is spring. The earth comes to life again and everyone who has been observing is made to consider the wonder, the power, and the goodness of the One Who created it all.

Working according to intricately designed laws, life-giving sap climbs to the very peak of the tallest trees to nourish the developing buds. Insects awake from their winter naps to pollinate the flowers, clean and fertilize the earth, and beautify the world with an endless variety of color and sound.

Who has considered why the birds sing at the break of day?

How many people have stood outdoors on a clear, dark night and stared up into the heavens—and wondered?

Modern science has added much to our knowledge of God. Among other things we have learned that the universe is composed of billions and billions of stars like our own sun, reaching out into space for billions upon billions of miles (or in scientific terms, light years).

The Bible tells us that at one time this world was without form and void, like a great abyss, until God created the beauties of our earth. According to the book of Genesis, this creation occurred during a short span of six days as God spoke and things came into being. Finally, as the last and crowning act of this creation, God made man. He made man after His own image and gave to him the dominion of this world to rule over it and to enjoy its beauty (Genesis 1:1-13).

Then to assure that man would remember his origin, He made the seventh day of that creation week a spe-

1. Isaiah 40:21-31 (NIV: "Do you not know? Have you not heard? Has it not been told you from the beginning? Have you not understood since the earth was founded? He sits enthroned above the circle of the earth, and its people are like grasshoppers. He stretches out the heavens like a canopy, and spreads them out like a tent to live in. He brings princes to naught and reduces the rulers of this world to nothing. No sooner are they planted, no sooner are they sown, no sooner do they take root in the ground, than he blows on them and they wither, and a whirlwind sweeps them away like chaff.

"'To whom will you compare me? Or who is my equal?' says the Holy one. Lift up your eyes and look to the heavens: Who created all these? He who brings out the starry host one by one, and calls them each by name. Because of his great power and mighty strength, not one of them is missing.

"Why do you say, O Jacob, and complain, O Isreal, 'My way is hidden from the Lord; my cause is disregarded by my God'? Do you not know? Have you not heard? The Lord is the ever lasting God, the Creator of the ends of the earth. He will not grow tired or weary, and his understanding no one can fathom. He gives strength to the weary and increases the power of the weak. Even youths grow tired and weary, and young men stumble and fall; but those who hope in the Lord will renew their strength. They will soar on wings like eagles; they will run and not grow weary, they will walk and not be faint."

2. Job 38:1-33 (NIV): "Then the Lord answered Job out of the storm. He said: "'Who is this that darkens my counsel with words without knowledge? Brace yourself like a man; I will question you, and you shall answer me. "'Where were you when I laid the earth's foundation? Tell me, if you understand. Who marked off its dimensions? Surely you know! Who stretched a measuring line across it? On what were its footings set, or who laid its cor-

cial time, a memorial of creation, a Holy Day when God and man might celebrate together the beauties of life (Genesis 2:1-3).

Over and over again throughout Scripture, God reiterates His claim that He is the creator and as creator He is above every other God (1, 2). It is by His authority as Creator that day follows day and night follows night and the earth continues its course around the sun. By the same authority, we are subject to Him as a little child is subject to loving parents.

It makes all the difference in the world what man believes about his origins. If one accepts the Biblical statement that God is creator, that He formed man out of the dust of the earth and gave life of His own breath, created man in His image to live in harmony with His universe to enjoy everlasting life—if one believes as the Bible also states that mankind forfeited the dominion of this earth when he yielded to the temptations of Satan and in essence joined in Satan's rebellion against God—if one believes the Bible contention that God is a loving God not willing that any should perish, and in fact, God loved man so much that He sent His only begotten son into the world to save him—if man believes these things, it will affect his whole behavior.

If, on the other hand, man is the product of an evolving line of creatures beginning as an accident on some primordial sea billions and billions of years ago, and the human experience is nothing more than one short step on a road to bigger and better things, lives will also be affected and behavior modified—but in a different way.

Of what purpose is the blood shed on the cross of Calvary if humans are creatures of evolution? Where is the incentive and the power to live victorious lives and overcome evil if all of the experiences in life are in reality necessary for the evolution of a higher being? Where are the moral absolutes that allow man to form valid beliefs about marriage and abortion and war and government if he is learning and evolving.

If the theory of evolution is true, then the message of the Bible must be a farce, and those who claim it as their moral code are living hypocrites or simple fools. In fact, if the Bible account of God is not as stated, i.e., that He is personally interested in this world and each individual, and if His word as spoken in Holy Writ is not to be understood and taken literally, then man really does not have a trustworthy, all-powerful Father upon whom he can lean when in need and to whom he can go with troubles and concerns. But where is there another source of real peace?

And if there is no such God, it is only natural that man makes his own gods, for he lives in a world that is obviously beyond human control and needs some god. To see that this is a valid argument, one need only look at the world today to note the many gods that man has made for himself—gods of power, of wealth, of pride, of education, gods of people, and gods of wood and stone. Programmed into each human being is the need for a god. And if the God of the Bible is not real, another will be found.

It is critical what each individual believes about creation and evolution. To take God at His word throughout the Holy Scripture, to accept the record of the fall and rebellion in sin, and the need for a Savior, costs much in terms of human pride and independence. Man does not like to be dependent—even upon God. He likes to be in control and run his own show. Belief in evolution allows him to do that. Creationism does not.

There is only one problem: God's way through dependency upon Him leads to life and health and harmony and happiness.

Every other way leads to death.

Look at the world of the twentieth century—a world where evolutionary theory dominates scientific thought. Technologically man has climbed to heights undreamed of even a generation ago. There now is the technological know-how to feed, clothe, and quench the thirst of every one in the whole earth; but instead of using this technology to serve each other, men have manufactured greater and greater arsenals whereby to destroy one another.

And even with the whole record of history and the ability to see how nation after nation has gone down to their ruin, man finds himself headed in the same direction and unable to solve the moral dilemmas of the present day.

Adventists believe that the fourteenth chapter of the book of Revelation provides God's answer to the problem. It is found in the warning call of the first angel to acknowledge and worship the One who created humans. Only after condescending from pedestals of self-sufficiency, both as individuals and as nations, and recognizing his dependency upon the God of crea-

nerstone—while the morning stars sang together and all the angels shouted for joy? Who shut up the sea behind doors when it burst forth from the womb, when I made the clouds its garment and wrapped it in thick darkness, when I fixed limits for it and set its doors and bars in place, when I said, "This far you may come and no farther; here is where your proud waves halt"? "'Have you ever given orders to the morning, or shown the dawn its place, that it might take the earth by the edges and shake the wicked out of it? The earth takes shape like clay under a seal; its features stand out like those of a garment. The wicked are denied their light, and their upraised arm is broken.

"'Have you journeyed to the springs of the sea or walked in the recesses of the deep? Have the gates of death been shown to you? Have you seen the gates of the shadow of death? Have you comprehended the vast expanses of the earth? Tell me, if you know all this.
"'What is the way to the abode of light? And where does darkness reside? Can you take them to their places? Do you know the paths to their dwellings? Surely you know, for you were already born! You have lived so many years!
"'Have you entered the storehouses of the snow or seen the storehouses of the hail, which I reserve for time of trouble, for days of war and battle? What is the way to the place where the lightning is dispersed, or the place where the east winds are scattered over the earth? Who cuts a channel for the torrents of rain, and a path for the thunderstorm, to water a land where no man lives, a desert with no one in it, to satisfy a desolate wasteland and make it sprout with grass? Does the rain have a father? Who fathers the drops of dew? From whose womb comes the ice? Who gives birth to the frost from the heavens when the waters become hard as stone, when the surface of the deep is frozen?
"'Can you bind the beautiful Pleiades? Can

tion can man expect the wisdom and the moral fortitude to change the downward course.

Adventists also believe that the human race is something special to Almighty God. They are His children by virtue of His creative love. He created the world for their enjoyment in all of its beauty and utility. When man fell, He risked all of heaven to rescue and restore man back to his original state. Even now, through the agency of the Holy Spirit and the ministry of the angels of heaven, He is actively engaged in His rescue mission. He will spare no expense short of recalling the God-given right of freedom and self-determination to accomplish His mission. In response to this kind of love, Adventists believe that there is no gift of gratitude too costly, no sacrifice too great to give in His honor.

Evolution provides no similar incentive by which to benefit the human race. It provides no example of the power inherent in self-sacrificing love. And it assures no solution to the destructive nature of human selfishness and pride.

Chapter XIII

The Paradox of Adventism: The Author's Testimony

In the pages of this book we have examined Adventism from the perspective of determining its place in religious reckoning. By careful examination of its origin, purpose for existence, and major controversial doctrinal beliefs, I have sought to clarify questions regarding its true nature. More specifically, does it deserve recognition as a positive religious force serving to bless and uplift the human race? Or does it tend to weaken and destroy that which is good in the world? Is it truly Christian? Or is it a cult?

We have noted that, to many, Adventism is a paradox. Adventists are recognized for their diligent study of the Scriptures, their missionary zeal, their emphasis on health and healing, and their attention to the poor and hurting people of the world. They are also noted for their exemplary use of the printed page and the electronic media in sharing the Gospel with the world. But they still present a paradox to many observers. With all of those qualities that speak well for their Creator and the Christ of the Gospel, most non-Adventists are comfortable. But the Adventist understanding and emphasis on such doctrines as the state of the dead and eternal punishment, the proper relationship between law and grace including the Sabbath, the authority of Scriptures, and the Adventist belief in the prophetic gift, are contrary to mainline Christianity. This paradox poses problems for many.

To the credit of the Gospel, many critics of Adventism have been honest and sincere in their evaluations. In their study of the Advent Movement, these have not always been able to come to a consensus or to resolve the conflicts and paradoxes. Why?

Adventists are a worldwide movement now numbering in the millions of believers. They do not have a written creed. They believe in a number of basic concepts and function in an organized fashion. They believe that truth is absolute, but can only be understood by human beings to the extent that God is able to make Himself known through the blindness caused by sin.

Adventist have often taught the concept of "present

truth." This concept means that certain teachings can only be understood, or have more relevance at one time in history than another depending on the circumstances then prevalent in the world. Thus, the emphasis for the last days of this world history may in many senses be different from other times. In fact, the emphasis upon a particular truth may vary even from year to year.

Furthermore, even among the fellowship of believers, the various facets of truth are not all understood with equal emphasis. Depending upon one's cultural heritage, hereditary and environmental factors, education, etc., each may see things slightly differently.

The Advent Movement allows for this variation. This is undoubtedly one of its strengths.

Because of this tolerance, however, a critic observing from outside the organized church may have difficulty identifying a clear consensus of doctrine (Lewis, 1966). Add to this the varying degrees of belief or unbelief demonstrated in the lives of professed believers, the task becomes even more formidable. Many are Adventists in name only and have wandered far from those basic tenets that established the Faith. Some, at the other extreme, are controlled by fanaticism.

Many Adventists recognize that they, like the wanton wife of Hosea, have wandered like other Christians after other lovers without completely forsaking Him to whom they profess to be married (Hosea 1:2-17). Likewise, they acknowledge that so far as the members of the Advent Movement have adulterated by whatever means the truths they profess, they are guilty to the world of onlookers for the confusion and paradox.

Fortunately, Adventists serve a God as exemplified by Hosea who forgives their transgressions and keeps calling them to His side. I pray that those who have been led astray by our waywardness may be similarly forgiving and look beyond our example to the beauties of the truths given to us to proclaim.

Seventh-day Adventists as a people, quite typical of human nature, take no great pleasure in being singled out for being different. The pejorative label "cult" is not a label that most of us would seek. In both sociological and theological terms, the word "cult" retains certain disparaging connotations. That Adventists have shed this term in the eyes of most of our critics leaves me with mixed emotions. I am concerned that in attempting to make our message acceptable, we may have been less than completely honest in the presentation we have made of this message to the world and thereby kept back truth that should have been heralded more clearly.

Closely related to this is the desire and concern that I share with those of my fellow believers who may be inclined to pass lightly over controversial issues. Our desire is that this message be made truly attractive so that its full beauty may be given opportunity to be seen—that it not be blocked prematurely by disparaging labels that might keep sincere seekers after truth from investigating for themselves.

While it is true that Adventists have at times appeared to be elitist or exclusive, I believe that the message of the Advent Movement is a message for all peoples and that the Advent believers themselves have no particular corner on God's love. Rather, they have been appointed as instruments, tools, vehicles, through which our loving God's last warning message to the world may be proclaimed in preparation for His return and the completion of His plan for the restoration of the fallen race.

I believe that the teachings of the Adventist faith represent a picture of God and His plan that is both very tenable to the eye of reason as well as in full compliance with the tenor of the Holy Scriptures. I believe that the concept of the Great Controversy Between Good and Evil as understood and proclaimed by the Adventist people is the only rational way to make sense of the many questions that arise in the human mind when confronted with the consequences of evil ever present in the world around us.

When understood in its basic components, one is given to understand that our Creator is indeed a God of infinite love and that love is a sufficiently powerful force to redeem and restore the fallen race and to forever eliminate any potential recurrence of the sin experience among His created universe.

Although it is true that even in the context of the Great Controversy there are questions eluding answers, it is clear that someone has those answers. At the proper time, they may all be understood.

I believe that the prophetic gift has been given by God for this particular time in history. The gift has not been given for an exclusive group of people, but for the whole human race. If at times members of the Adventist Movement have improperly emphasized the writings of Ellen White and placed them in other than their intended role (and this certainly has been done), this must not detract from their value nor their source.

If God has used Ellen White, then I would be a fool to reject His voice just because someone else may discredit the messenger.

For myself, I have tested the writings of Ellen White and have found them a source of inspiration, direction, and encouragement, all entirely in keeping with the teachings of the Holy Scriptures.

Specifically, as a physician, I have thrilled as I have seen counsels written more than one hundred years ago now confirmed by valid scientific research. Such things would not have been possible by human invention alone.

Of similar interest is the fulfillment of the predictions that were written regarding the final events that were destined to occur before the return of our Lord: I refer to the specific statements regarding the unification of the religious world under the banner of Sunday sacredness. Even thirty years ago this prediction was acceptable only by faith. Today few knowledgeable with the world around them can fail to see its development and imminent fulfillment.

While I believe that the Sabbath as a doctrine is of primary importance as a vehicle through which the human and divine develop a relationship, it is becoming increasingly evident that the Sabbath will also be, as predicted, a test by which the true and the counterfeit believers may be distinguished.

For those who are tempted to doubt this statement, may I suggest a careful reading of the book, *The Great Controversy Between Christ and Satan,* by Ellen G. White, comparing its statements to the daily religious news. The accusation by some that Adventism is guilty of misinterpreting the authority of Scripture because of our belief in the prophetic gift through Ellen White is, based upon present evidence, I believe, unfounded.

Regarding obedience to law, Adventists are considered legalistic by many not only because of the Sabbath commandment but also because of their belief and teaching that the laws of health are laws of cause and effect and that obedience is a response of love to the Creator who instituted those laws. As a matter of fact, I believe that all law is indeed summed up in the two Great Commandments: "Thou shalt love the Lord your God with all your heart, and soul, and mind, and your neighbor as yourself" (Mark 12:29, 30). For when love as it occurs when Christ Jesus dwells within is expressed in all of its beauty and purity, when this law of love is written on the heart as Scripture describes, then everything that one does or does not do is under that controlling principle of love. It is no longer, therefore, a legalistic requirement but is a thing of willingness and joy. Yet, much of the Christian world fails to comprehend this truth and, therefore, must seek other means to explain the relationship that exists between faith and works.

There is one other point of difference that sets Adventists apart from any other Christians. It is the status of the dead and the doctrine of eternal torment. After studying this doctrine thoroughly in Scripture and examining the historical origin, I believe that the evidence favors the Adventist belief that man became a living being when God breathed into him the breath of life, and that when man dies his life ceases and the breath (nothing more) returns to God who gave it.

In the final resurrection the righteous will be raised to life again into the image of God; the wicked will be resurrected so as to understand the consequences of the choice which they have made in rejecting God's loving calls to their hearts and to acknowledge the love, goodness, and justice of God in pronouncing His judgment.

In this context, when the plan is complete, sin and sinners have been finally dealt with in true love and with full respect for individual freedom, then the harmony and the peace and the joy in the universe present before sin marred God's creation will again be restored in all of its beauty.

This kind of religion makes sense to my mind. I am able to understand in this context that love is love and not hate, and that God is God and not a devil. I am able to see purpose and cause and effect even in the sadness and pain that I experience in the world around me. My heart rejoices and praises the God who has revealed Himself so beautifully to me.

If by espousing this kind of a God and this type of faith, people question my relationship with my God and choose to call me by disparaging terms, and call the movement which is the very warp and woof of my being a "cult," then I must join those of the faithful through all the ages who have accepted ridicule and embarrassment, exclusion and persecution, yes, and even death itself as the price for following my Master.

Are Adventists a cult? The reader must decide. In the pages of this book I have not settled the issue to the satisfaction of all. I hope that I have provided sufficient evidence whereby honest people may decide. I also hope that I have stimulated many to search deeply into the Scriptures under the guiding influence of the Holy Spirit to find truth for themselves.

John 8:32: "You shall know the truth, and the truth will set you free."

REFERENCES

Lewis, Gordon R. The Bible, The Christian, and the Seventh-day Adventists. *Grand Rapids, MI: Baker Book House, 1966.*

White, Ellen G. The Great Controversy Between Christ and Satan. *Mountain View, CA:Pacific Press Publishing Association, 1950.*

Bibliography

Adventist Review. Hagerstown, Maryland: Review and Herald Publishing Association.

Bacchiocchi, Samuele. *From Sabbath to Sunday.* Rome: The Pontifical Gregorian Press, 1977.

Coltheart, Elder J. F. *The Sabbath of God Through the Centuries.* Payson, Arizona: Leaves-of-Autumn Books, Inc., 1954.

Fudge, Edward William. *The Fire that Consumes.* Houston, Texas: Providential Press, 1982.

Guy, Fritz. "Eternity in Time." *Adventist Review.* Washington, D.C.: Review and Herald Publishers, May 28, 1987.

McMillen, S.I., M.D. *None of These Diseases.* Westwood, New Jersey: Fleming H. Revell Company, 1963.

Maxwell, C. Mervyn, Ph.D. *God Cares, Vol. 2.* Boise, Idaho: Pacific Press Publishing Association, 1985.

Nelson, Ethel R. and Broadberry, Richard E. *Mysteries Confucius Couldn't Solve.* Lancaster, Maine: Read Books Publisher, 1986.

Seiss, Joseph A. *The Gospel in the Stars.* Grand Rapids, Michigan: Kregel Publications, 1972.

Strand, Kenneth A., editor. *The Sabbath in Scripture and History.* Washington, D.C.: Review and Herald Publishing Association, 1982.

Thompson, Walter C., M.D. *Pearls and Pills.* Amherst, Wisconsin: Palmer Publications, 1986.

White, Ellen. Washington D.C. and Hagerstown, Maryland: Review and Herald Publishing Association. Also, Mountain View, California: Pacific Press Publishing Association.

The Great Controversy Between God and Satan, 1888.
The Desire of Ages, 1898.
Education, 1903.
The Ministry of Healing, 1905.
Steps to Christ, 1908.
Counsels on Diet and Foods, 1938.
Thoughts from the Mount of Blessings, 1956.

Wilkinson, Benjamin George, Ph.D. *Truth Triumphant.* Payson, Arizona: Leaves-of-Autumn Books, 1944.

Wisbrock, George. *Death and the Soul After Life.* Published by George Wisbrock, 1986.